STAY TRUE TO YOU

A.J. TRANTER

ISBN

978-1-916606-04-3 (Paperback)
978-1-916606-03-6 (E-book)

Editing, cover art, and book design by PaperTrue Ltd.

Printed in United Kingdom

First edition on August 2020

Published by PaperTrue
Market Street, Suite 1300, San Francisco, CA 94111.
https://www.papertrue.com

Contents

Foreword

My ongoing journey of healing from trauma inspired me to write this book. When I was quarantined for a long period during the COVID-19 pandemic, I began my journey of inner healing. I am a design engineer in the transportation industry; my job allows me to work from home. Further, as I have been living in a shared accommodation, I have had plenty of time to reflect on all that was happening. When I was quarantined, I had to find alternate ways to connect with people instead of meeting them face-to-face.

So, I turned to social media platforms and joined groups on Facebook related to personality types and Spirituality. I also interacted on private WhatsApp groups where the members were interested in Spirituality and Self-Healing. It was a diverse group where people expressed their innermost feelings. I must have found the right groups because everything that was posted heavily resonated with me. I started interacting with more people, and it was comforting to know that I could talk to people in the comfort of my house. However, communicating over the internet couldn't replace face-to-face interactions. One of the groups I ended up joining was a yoga community that concentrated on trauma healing by activating the seven chakras of the body, which was not initially something

I was interested in. The journey ultimately took a highly spiritual turn. I have been a Christian for 13 years now, so I was already aware of the spiritual realm; however, I ventured further into areas I didn't know existed. While all this was going on, I did take a close look at my friends and family, and the pandemic clearly showed me who was there for me and who wasn't. At this point, I had to re-evaluate my relationships and start with a fresh mind-set by choosing the people I would spend time with once the pandemic was over. It was a wise decision on my part since I started to feel less apprehensive around certain people, and over time, I gradually started to surround myself with the right people, and I'm incredibly grateful for that.

A friend of mine noticed my growth as I healed from my trauma and learned how to take care of my mental health. The growth resulted in my increased confidence and passion, and I was able to manifest the things I wanted and break free from the depressive and anxious cycles that I didn't even realise I was trapped in. A friend of mine recommended that I write a book, but I didn't believe I had the necessary writing skills to do so. After spending some time thinking about what to write, I began jotting down some content and found myself becoming more interested. I knew that if I wrote all the content I wanted, I could have it edited to make the wording more effective and professional. Before I knew it, I had a book. Knowing that I was able to achieve this, I hope that my book can serve as a testimony to those who have a goal but are concerned that they lack the ability to reach it. They should not allow their doubts or fears to hinder them from achieving their goals.

This book will touch on various topics to motivate you, including how the yoga community assisted me in beginning my trauma healing and how I acquired some enduring skills that help me deal with challenges from all aspects of my life. The aim of this book is to inspire you to take a stand against those who consistently bring pain and grief in your life, as well as breaking free from regular painful cycles you experience in your life, whether that's at home, at work, with family or with friends. This book also aims to remind you of your worth as an individual. I interacted with many people who too were healing from their pain and transforming into wonderful and powerful versions of themselves. I will draw on a variety of sources that I find interesting, including the Bible, films, TV shows, music, books and personal stories to illustrate my points. It's okay if not all of them resonate with you. The goal is to help you grow and strengthen yourself, so you can pick and choose anything that resonates more with you and apply it to your life the way you see fit. I'll be discussing a variety of topics that I hope will be interesting to you and provide you with some thought-provoking nuggets that will help you realise your full potential, get rid of any restricting negative attitudes and not only realise but also remember that you are undeniably and wonderfully unique. To all of those who read this book I want to say that you should know you are special. You have a distinctive personality; your tastes, interests, talents and your story are your own, and all of these have shaped you into the unique person that you are.

AJ Tranter
July 2022

Acknowledgements

I owe my gratitude to everyone who supported and encouraged me throughout the writing of this book, which was a Herculean task.

I would like to express my gratitude to someone who has played a significant role in my growth and development. Nat Riley of the Empath Academy reached out to me through Facebook and invited me to join her community. She revealed to me that I was an Empath (which I didn't know at that time), that I had gifts that could be further cultivated and that I had the potential to achieve more than what I imagined I could. She provided me with a lot of resources to improve my life and heal from my past trauma. She helped me make some great developments and gave me the mental strength to survive the pandemic. Her guidance has left a lasting impact on me; it shall always be remembered.

As a devout Christian, my faith has also played a crucial role in my journey. Reading the Bible gives me peace of mind, and a lot of my core values and beliefs derive from the numerous Bible studies that I've undertaken with fellow practicing Christians. During the pandemic, I read several books on Christianity to find solace and further my understanding of my faith. The books provided me with wisdom and kept me mentally active through periods of isolation. I'm aware that not all readers will be interested in religion or faith; therefore, I'll only be sharing a few ideas that were helpful to me. It is ultimately your choice whether to embrace these ideas or not.

I am also grateful to have a friend who has been there for me every step of the way. My best friend Georgia James is someone who I met in 2017 at work, and she has remained in contact with me ever since. We both began self-healing at roughly the same time but in different ways. Georgia has been a clear and absolute definition of a great friend; she encouraged me to let go of my negative thoughts, spent a lot of quality time with me, accepted me for who I was and has consistently shown interest in my life. She stood as a strong pillar of support whilst I wrote this book; I continue to have her unwavering support, and we have always helped each other through thick and thin. Throughout our journey towards healing, we both helped each other, which has allowed us to learn some profound truths about ourselves. Even if the truths have been upsetting, they have enabled us to make the biggest breakthroughs. Georgia is the kind of amazing, wonderful friend who I believe everyone needs in their life.

During the pandemic lockdowns, I read several books by different authors, and I believe they deserve thanks for the valuable insight and wisdom they offered, equipping me with practical skills to confront life's toughest challenges. For those of you who are interested in the sources and want to look up the authors, a list of the books I read to assist me in writing this book has been included at the end of this book.

Finally, I'd like to thank even those who have come and gone from my life, who made my life difficult and uncomfortable and who caused me grief or pain. A key life lesson for me is that it's through our failures that we grow stronger. I wouldn't have been forced to recover if the ones who hurt me hadn't provided me with the opportunities to grow and strengthen myself. No one enjoys suffering, but I can assure you that it helps us become stronger and better versions of ourselves. Even though most of these people are not present in my life right now, I believe they have served a purpose.

01. In Your Family

1.1. WHAT IS FAMILY?

The term 'family' has traditionally been defined as a group of people consisting of one or two parents and their children living together as a cohesive unit. While that is true, family can also mean more than just that. I have personally defined family as the group of people you can trust and depend on in every situation because of the great love they give you, regardless of whether they are blood-related or not. Families are never easy to talk about, but they are also something we cannot do without. We all come from families; different cultures have different notions of what an ideal family should be like. What does an ideal family look like to you is a big topic to start the discussion with. In other words, what would you anticipate from family members in terms of their actions, how they would interact with you, the environment they would create and the love that they would demonstrate? Since we use the term "family" to refer to the people we spend the most time with or have emotionally invested in the most, I think that family is where we expect to be loved the most. I'm sure that if we placed people from all around the world in one room and asked them what family means to them, we would get a wide range of responses. Regardless of all the responses we may get, I believe they would all mention the concept of being loved. Given the vast diversity of human experience and the multitude of cultures that have existed throughout history, it is possible that there are many ideas that are unfamiliar to us or that challenge our expectations. While some of these ideas may seem extreme or unusual, it is important to acknowledge that there is much that we may not yet understand about the world and the people who inhabit it.

Deep down in our hearts, all of us yearn for a family - a place where we feel respected and where we can reasonably expect to receive happiness from our loved ones. In a world where we can sometimes feel insignificant and misunderstood, we expect our family to show us great compassion and understanding. Every person yearns for a family, but unfortunately, over time, different conceptions of what a family should look like have evolved across cultures, and when we examine some of them closely, we may think, "This is not what I expect a family to look like." Perhaps in some cultures or nations families do things differently. However, one need not look at other cultures or nations. Everywhere, families are meant to be the torchbearers of community traditions and guides for individual members to undertake certain activities that manifest unity among the community and family members. Some family traditions in our society are well-known, such as holiday get-togethers, praying before meals, game nights, celebrating life milestones, film nights and annual trips to a particular place.

Many traditions such as christenings, baptisms, fasting and mass gatherings at churches that celebrate a holiday or event, have religious roots. Every family has their views about how to live their lives. Families come in all shapes and sizes. Depending on a person's circumstances, a family may consist of parents and children, husband and wife, one parent and one or more children, aunts and uncles and their children, grandparents and their grandchildren, only siblings and people with adopted family members. Some family circles may even converge or refer to one another as "family friends" when referring to people who are close to them. Families can consist of as many people as desired; there's no limit.

Every family is unique and has its own individual culture, and we should try to understand their culture before passing any judgements, especially if they haven't given you the full picture of their current situation. Families can now be created by adoption, blood relations or by signing a legal contract. Do any of your friends, who don't fall into one of the three aforementioned groups, feel like family to you? With the love and affection they showed you, the gifts they gave you and the journey you've shared, do you feel that they were just like the family member you had always wanted? Lately, I have encountered individuals who are not connected to me by blood or law; yet due to their affection and empathy towards me, I regard them as my family. They helped me see what a family member looks like and gave me new perspectives on what a family is. Perhaps you have some friends who treat you with the same level of affection as family members.

To summarise, I believe that unconditional love is the foundation of a true family, where everyone helps each other out without expecting anything in return.

If your blood relatives or friends accept you for who you are, you will feel secure with one another. You will listen to each other without judgement or insults, feel valued and appreciated, and not feel the need to hide any aspect of yourself. On top of that, if you find yourself in danger, they will recognise your situation and rush to help you through the storm. They are always there for you whenever you cry for help. The following quote from a Disney film perfectly captures the meaning of the Hawaiian term for family:

Ohana means family, family means nobody
gets left behind or forgotten.
(Lilo and Stitch, 2002)

Do you believe that this is what a family looks like? Can you say that this quote reflects your family? Think about it.

1.2. OPINIONS OF FAMILY MEMBERS

Just like how everyone is born with a unique body, each one of us has a unique mind. This inevitably means that despite all the things you do together as a family, you will have your own opinions and views on a variety of topics.

This means that there will undoubtedly be arguments as well as disagreements. It's okay to hold different opinions from one another. After all, we weren't programmed to like the same things just like how we weren't designed to look the same either. Otherwise, there would be no such thing as diversity or uniqueness. So, what happens when there are disagreements within the family? Either the disagreements are resolved peacefully, or they lead to very heated arguments and actions. While raising us, our parents had their values, beliefs and opinions on how they should raise us. When very young, babies will imitate and learn from their parents. I've witnessed several times where a parent does an action with a particular object in hand, and even if the child may not have the object within their grasp, they try to imitate their parent's actions.

When you have a child of your own, it is important to understand that they will learn new things as they grow older. But who do they learn from? It's from their parents. Since children assume that everything their parents do is good, they will essentially try to mimic their behaviour unless instructed otherwise. As children, we were taught to respect our parents (not all kids follow this, though). Parents discipline their children to bring them up in a certain way. To learn, our only choice as children was to imitate our parents' behaviour. As a result, a lot of our perceptions about the world are influenced by how our parents interacted with us, including how they made us feel. The habits we pick up and some of the behaviour we exhibit in our daily lives are the results of years of learning from our parent's behaviour.

Discipline may come across as a harsh word, but it is actually a helpful practise in our lives. Discipline has been defined as the act of obeying orders and adhering to a certain code of conduct, especially after being disobedient. Whilst it may seem restrictive, discipline can actually help us grow into more responsible and caring people. Examples of healthy discipline include eating regular meals throughout the day without skipping any, maintaining a clean and organised home or workplace to ensure a safe and visually appealing environment, and adhering to recommended sleep hours to avoid sleep deprivation or oversleeping.

Discipline is beneficial since it encourages us to act morally and mature into responsible adults. However, it isn't discipline if parents consistently pressure their children to act a certain way or fit their mould rather than allowing them to express their genuine personalities and interests. This will feel more like control than discipline. Control involves making someone act or behave in a certain way, whereas discipline is proper parenting. The distinction is obvious.

Gaslighting is a common form of coercion that involves convincing people that their reality, perceptions and sanity are not real and that having opinions of their own is wrong. It's not just common amongst families but it can also happen in school with classmates or bullies, at work with colleagues or in social circles when an individual who doesn't get along with you may despise you. Any one of the people you regularly encounter in your life may try to impose their style on others, so it can happen anywhere.

Here are a few examples of what someone gas lighting you may look like: convincing you that a problem you're having isn't really a problem, lying to you despite the truth being right in front of them, telling you that you're "overreacting" or "imagining things" when you're upset, talking over you and, worst of all, projecting their problems onto you (where if this person is abusing you, they will say you are abusing them). There will come a time when we will mature, have our own opinions and beliefs and discover that our beliefs differ from those of our parents. What makes sense to you will be the determining factor in your ability to distinguish between your opinions and those of your parents. It's a sign that you don't believe something if your thoughts conflict with what you like or what makes sense to you. When growing up, at one point, you will likely tell your parents about your likes and dislikes. You will voice out about what brings you discomfort. Not all outcomes can be predicted, but parents will either pay attention and accept your beliefs or they will immediately dismiss them.

Without a doubt, not being listened to can lead to sadness and depression. All of us want to be heard and not ignored. Some parents (or the ones who have the responsibility of bringing up a child) disregard their children's opinions and enforce their beliefs on them because they believe that they know what is best for their children. Parents often make the best decisions for their children, but they're not always right. They are human like everyone else and make mistakes. Those who claim to be without fault are lying to themselves (The Bible - 1 John 1:8). It may be difficult for some to accept this reality, but it makes sense that we all make mistakes occasionally. When we are young, we can hold onto the belief that we're wrong a lot of the time if we've experienced a lot of gas lighting. As a result, when our true interests show up, we may prioritise our parent's interests over our own. This may happen because we have an inner voice that tells us that our parents' opinions are always correct.

Once we recognise that our parents' beliefs and opinions may not be consistent with what we learn from the world around us, it is essential to start questioning and evaluating them based on their alignment with reality. When we voice our beliefs and opinions to our parents, they may either listen and acknowledge them out of love or they will ignore them out of spite. You can imagine how painful and scary the latter would be, especially if the parent suffers from a feeling of insecurity or has a tendency to become aggressive when challenged. You and your parents may agree on many things, which is great; however, the greatest challenge concerns how disagreements among family are handled. This will be covered in detail later in this chapter.

1.3. FEELINGS AND REACTIONS

As previously stated, you can imagine how frightening it must be when family members argue, leading to yelling, anger and occasional violence. When our parents abuse us as children, it can seem more terrifying than words can really express. So, when we feel unsafe, we naturally wonder where else we can find safety. We ask ourselves many questions like: What did I do? Why are they doing this to me? Am I that bad? Will the abuse end? And so on. No one wants to feel scared. The worst-case scenario is when someone fears their fear, and this may cause an emotional downward spiral.

I agree. Feeling scared can be a frightening experience, and as humans and vulnerable creatures, we often try to live our lives in ways that minimise our exposure to scary situations, especially during childhood. When we were babies, we had no understanding of what fear and violence were. We were fascinated by everything around us, and we would go around exploring everything by touching it. Babies often touch objects that their parents don't want them to. Parents don't want babies to touch certain objects for various reasons; sometimes, it's for safety reasons, like avoiding an open flame or a live socket, and other times it's for more personal reasons. By disciplining children in the right way, they can be taught what is acceptable and what is not. However, an aggressive tone instils fear into children and will cause irreparable mental and emotional damage. The damage is greater when physical abuse and mishandling come into play, and the consequence is a child who lives in constant fear. This is especially true if there isn't any emotional understanding and compassion to make up for the fear that was driven into them.

When we experience a scary situation, our nervous systems go into something called the "fight-or-flight" mode. Another name for this is the Sympathetic mode. Some call it the "fight, flight or freeze" mode because one of the three scenarios can happen: we try to attack the threat in an attempt to put an end to it, we run away so that the threat can't catch us or we remain incredibly still in the hopes that the threat will go away. The Sympathetic mode was the regular term that was used when practising self-healing with the Empath Academy. This is most likely how we typically respond to threats from our parents and other similar situations. A similar undesirable situation is when we injure ourselves while in fight mode. This doesn't mean that we hate ourselves or like the pain. No one likes pain! People try to cope with their suffering by developing destructive habits, but this rarely works. (I learnt this from an author and YouTube video creator named Teal Swan, whose videos were very insightful for my self-healing). The opposite of the sympathetic mode is the para-sympathetic mode, also known as the "rest-and-digest" mode. This is a situation in which we don't feel threatened or endangered, and we can relax.

As humans, we like familiarity; the fear of the unknown is something that everyone experiences.

Therefore, when people deal with a problem for a long period, they become accustomed to it and are not aware of the potential damage that may result from the coping mechanism. As a result, individuals may hesitate to choose a course or path that is substantially different from what they are used to because they prefer to continue with what they know. It's not the agony people desire to endure; rather, it's a coping strategy they employ to lessen their suffering or fulfil their needs. Therefore, it's important to keep in mind that people aren't attached to pain or suffering in any way. In a typical house, there aren't many places to hide as a child. This restricts the child's opportunity to flee from a threat (flight mode). I haven't yet heard of any kids who fought back when their parents yelled at them. It's not surprising that the parent's authority, stature and tone would be sufficient to subconsciously convince the young child that fighting back is forbidden. There's nothing wrong with voicing out your emotions and feelings. We ALL have them. It doesn't seem like an act of love if parents condemn their children for expressing their honest feelings. I'll say it again, your emotions are valid, and you have the right to express how you feel, provided the manner in which it's done is healthy. A loving family will acknowledge your feelings and make you feel valued.

It's important to pay attention to the reactions we get from angry parents who disagree with us. Knowing that your feelings are valid, despite how your parents respond is the first and most important thing to do. Your feelings matter, and its okay to be vulnerable. To have a deep relationship, one must be vulnerable. You don't have to be vulnerable with everyone, especially not with those who disregard your emotions. Since you do spend time outside your house, I can guarantee that there will be some people out there who will want to acknowledge your feelings.

1.4. MY EXPERIENCE WITH MY FAMILY

In this section, I will share some of my personal experiences with family. I believe that sharing this will shed some light on global events that take place in the real world. I experienced several different kinds of abuse (mental and physical) and neglect from my family. It was without a doubt a terrifying environment to grow up in.

I was physically abused by one family member when I was a child, and I was raised to believe that this was typical of family upbringing. I had the impression that it was a family member's responsibility to physically abuse the child into submission whenever a mistake was made. I used to think I was incompetent when I got screamed at for making minor mistakes. When I was a child, it seemed like the only time I ever received praise was when I did a job well. The pattern that resulted from this was that I developed a belief that the only way to receive love was to perform a task flawlessly. (You can imagine how challenging that can be in today's world.) It was dreadful to witness the way the family disintegrated with the divorce of my parents. The divorce happened soon after a move across the country. From there, going between two homes in a typical week wasn't exactly simpler; I continued to receive frequent abuse from one family member while receiving emotional deafness from another. I was under a lot of pressure to do well in my academics because it was highly expected of me. The majority of the time, I didn't know who to share my emotional problems with since I felt like they would be laughed at or discarded. I pretty much suffered in silence as I didn't speak up about any of the abuse I received. I felt like I had to earn love from my family members because of their long list of expectations, as opposed to love being freely given to me. While my family members provided for my physical needs like food and shelter, they did not meet my emotional needs.

Furthermore, even though they were emotional needs, they are nonetheless significant. We will experience the same issues that have repeatedly arisen throughout human history if we continue to act as though emotional needs are not all that important, with no one actually taking steps to address the issue that is occurring both in and around us. My family expected the following from me: always being the one to initiate conversations, keeping the house incredibly clean, putting my family first despite any mistreatment, doing well in academics, mirroring my parent's emotions, and everything is alright. I was drifting away from my actual feelings, my convictions and ultimately my true personality while I tried to live up to all these expectations. I sought approval from my family by compromising my true self, instead of attracting those who would accept me as I am. It was very clear that I would never be able to satisfy my family, and I had forgotten the truth that one cannot satisfy everyone. I spent over 26 years trying to please my parents before I started my self-healing journey.

When the COVID-19 pandemic struck, I stayed at home, as I could work remotely. I couldn't see my family during the pandemic because we lived on different sides of the country. This gave me a lot of time and space to reflect on my life. I used social media to connect with people and search for groups I could socialise with to satisfy my craving for intimacy. The leader of a yoga community that prioritised both physical and mental health sought me out in a group that suited my personality. Although I had plenty of free time, I was initially hesitant to join. However, I eventually gave in because I had nothing to lose. Throughout the pandemic, I enrolled myself in the group's courses, and before I knew it, I was discovering things about myself that I had never imagined, let alone realised. I discovered some unsettling truths, but I also gained some insights that helped me gain a better understanding of the life I live. It felt amazing to be rediscovering my true self. I was also becoming aware of how my family and friends were treating me. In all honesty, I didn't want to accept the reality of how I was being treated, but the good thing about this was that a huge burden was lifted off my shoulders, and all the uncertainties I had started to dissipate because some of my early assumptions had been proven correct. All along, I kept asking myself, "Why can't I have that?" as I put up with the abuse my family heaped on me, even when I watched others received love, compassion and understanding from their families. My coach taught me what genuine love in a family and friendship looks like. I saw examples of humility, recognition of emotions on both sides of a relationship, patience and understanding of one's feelings. In the classes hosted by my coach at Empath Academy, everyone demonstrated understanding and compassion by giving each other compliments, validation and comfort.

These made me clearly distinguish between who was giving me the love and compassion that I needed and who wasn't. My coach taught me techniques to make the healing process enjoyable so that it wasn't just hard work. I read books that were recommended to me, practised meditating on the Bible and engaged in fun activities to get to know myself. One book that aided my healing journey and helped me comprehend the emotional neglect of my family was "Adult Children of Emotionally Immature Parents" by Lindsay C. Gibson. I gained valuable insights into what emotional immaturity looks like within families, the psychological impact it has on children and how one can work towards healing from the wounds inflicted by one's parents.

Eventually, I reached a point where I was prepared to confront my family regarding their treatment of me. I will guide on this aspect later in the book. I spoke to each family member individually to gauge their reactions, and it was an interesting experience. My aim wasn't to fix anything but to express my opinions and reveal my true self to them. It wasn't a smooth process, and it put me in an emotionally challenging place as I faced the truth, but in the end, it was well worth it. I remained true to myself, and I no longer felt pressured to please people. I took care of myself to heal from the disputes, and now I feel more comfortable with who I am - body, mind and spirit. A fun fact: I love American sitcoms, and during my recovery from the dispute, I was recommended "Brooklyn Nine-Nine". I binge-watched the episodes in chronological order, and I must say that the show helped me get through a tough emotional time. The show is fantastic, in my opinion, I now hold it close to me, as it provided the light heartedness I needed along with the confidence to seek the right friends and ask for their help.

1.5. REVIEW YOUR FAMILY BELIEFS

We can't entirely hold our parents responsible for how they treated us in the past. They likely experienced trauma themselves that they have not yet healed from. Intergenerational trauma is a common and recurring phenomenon where the trauma experienced by one generation is passed down to the next. This pattern can continue for many generations, and it may be challenging to identify the origin of the initial trauma, but I'm sure if you talk to older relatives you might be able to get a wider picture of how some traits can be passed down within a family.

In some cultures, physical punishment is a part of disciplining children, including beatings or even using a stick. Of course, I believe any form of physical violence is disheartening; this is not how we should be treating one another. Human history is replete with examples of slavery, where entire races were sold into bondage and subjected to severe, terrifying and inhumane treatment methods. People were subjected to brutal physical punishment as a means of control and forced to work day in and day out. (They were inhumanely mistreated). Although we hope and pray that today is not like it was centuries ago, it's important to acknowledge that the trauma experienced by these slaves has likely been carried down through the generations. This phenomenon is known as ancestral trauma; where the trauma experienced by our ancestors is passed down to the next generations.

For instance, if a child experiences a particular pattern of abuse during their upbringing, such as manipulation, submission or physical beating, they may carry the emotional scars into adulthood if left unhealed. When it comes to having children of their own, they may feel a sense of release by manipulating or hurting their own children and forcing them to submit to their authority. In a sense, the parent may feel that their abuse has been materialised or noticed because their child is experiencing it in the same way they did.

As humans, when we experience pain, we never want to endure it alone. We would want someone to notice our cries for help. Sometimes, people cope with their pain by inflicting it upon others, to make them understand or to feel less alone in their suffering. This sometimes leads to revenge-seeking behaviour, where they aim to give their abuser a taste of their own medicine. Deep down, we all hope that others will understand the pain we're going through; as it assures us that we are not alone in our suffering. If you're interested in getting to know your family's beliefs and seeing how they align with yours, asking them questions and listening to their story is a great starting point. Hopefully, they will be open to sharing their story with you, and you may gain a better understanding of where they came from and all that they've been through. For whatever reason, some people might be reluctant to fully share their experiences, and that's okay; we need to respect their right to privacy. We may not be able to know the full story of our parents, but we can try our best to get the information. To be very clear, a traumatic past should not be an excuse to inflict pain upon others. Where would justice be if everyone claimed a history of abuse as a justification for hurting others? Additionally, since the past is in the past, we are not required to utilise any aspect of it to determine who we are. The best use of our past is to improve ourselves by using what we've learnt from it. As a famous quote from the Disney film "The Lion King" states:

The past can hurt. But the way I see it, you can either run from it, or learn from it.
(The Lion King, 1994)

Your family may not express their beliefs or history in words, but there is a different way to gather information that, in my opinion, will speak louder than words: observe their actions. Your childhood story is not an illusion. You should not let anyone convince you otherwise. Your childhood shaped and moulded you into the person you are today. Many of our actions as adults stem from our childhood experiences. Therefore, for any significant memories you remember, acknowledge them and have confidence in their existence. What do you remember about the way your parents treated you? Did you try to express yourself? Did they try to silence you? Did they pay attention to your emotions? Did they give you the space for self-expression? What methods did they use to bring you up? Now, if you were to confront your parents about the way they may have mistreated you, they will come up with a case to defend themselves and present themselves as the innocent party.

However, when it comes to causing damaged feelings, insults, criticism, abuse or any kind of inflicted pain, the person who inflicted the pain MUST take responsibility for their actions. No one can be held responsible for their behaviour except themselves. One of two scenarios can occur when confronting our parents about the way they treated us. They may be receptive to accepting responsibility for their actions, or they may be in denial and reject all suggestions concerning them being in the wrong. Some may go to extreme lengths to avoid admitting their mistakes, and in such cases, forcing an answer out of them may not be possible.

1.6. CHOOSING FAMILY

Family is not limited to blood relations. A family can be extended without any blood connections through marriage and adoption. While legal documentation is required to support these relationships, it is clear that individuals can become part of a family through these legal means. Some people even just like to use compliments like "This person is like family to me" and "This person is a family friend". Christian churches often emphasise the importance of being a united family, as members are encouraged to consider each other as "one body under Christ" (The Bible - Romans 12:5). As believers in the same God, churches should treat each other as family and be united in love rather than lies and violence. As for those who do not believe in God, even though there are many races around the world, we are all part of the human race. We're all human beings navigating our way through this chaotic world, and we can't traverse it alone. You'll be surprised at how multiple problems can be solved at once when everyone helps each other out. An example: two people who may be feeling lonely and looking for a friend can find solace in each other, thereby solving two problems at once.

Even when praying the Lord's Prayer, believers of God refer to him as "Our Father in Heaven" (The Bible - Matthew 6:9). We can choose to invite people from all over the world into our family. I strongly believe that the happiest and strongest of families are the ones that are united in love. I enjoy going to comic cons. I attend these events to connect with like-minded individuals who share my love for popular franchises and fandom's. Over time, I've met many wonderful people in the comic con community and formed deep, intimate relationships with them. We express ourselves and inspire each other with positivity and entertainment. We are undoubtedly connected by our shared passion for Marvel films, and even outside of comic cons, we provide each other with a lot of support. The love and kindness that I have received from these individuals have given me the family-level emotional connection I have been seeking.

The theme of family is evident in the Marvel franchise, particularly in the relationships between the characters from "The Avengers" and "Guardians of the Galaxy." Despite not being related to one another by blood, these characters work together, fight together and refer to each other as family on numerous occasions. This gave me great comfort because it implied that if I wanted to look for a family in the outside world like the heroes did, I could find one if I looked really hard, but I must remain true to myself.

I like to think of the friends I made at comic con events as my "comic con family" because they provide a safe and supportive space for me to be my true self. Our reunions, connections, compassion, kindness and love are just as intimate and meaningful as those experienced by biological families. Family should be a place of love, comfort and safety. It should be a place where you can trust the individuals who make up the circle and where you can be accepted for who you are, regardless of differences in opinion. If this kind of support and connection is not available within your biological family, it is perfectly acceptable to reach out to others outside the family and build meaningful relationships with them. If your biological family condemns you for wanting to seek connections outside the family, you mustn't take to heart their criticism. You shouldn't be controlled by those who make your family. Your family can consist of whomever you choose, whether they are your friends or your partner, as long as there is mutual agreement and everyone feels loved.

1.7. WHAT TO DO IN FAMILY SITUATIONS?

So, what will happen the next time there's a dispute in your family, and you want to stand up for what you truly believe in? Will you be worried about how your family will treat you when you speak your truth? Is there a part of you that fears what they might say or do to you? Will they make you feel so guilty that you will feel like you have no choice but to submit to their beliefs? It's a scary step, especially if your parents have previously reacted in a way that has scared you. Your mind recalls how terrifying that experience was, and you don't want to relive it. It's natural to experience fear and it's common to fear the fear itself. Embracing and acknowledging these feelings can help us better understand and overcome them. The antidote to fear is love. When you allow fear to grow inside of you, it quickly takes over your body and mind and becomes an always-on response as far as you are concerned. You need to replace the fear in your mind with love. Regardless of whether your parents listen to you or not, give yourself credit for the courageous move you're about to make. Not all parents may listen, but those who do will appreciate you for who you are. If you encounter opposition, remember your own strength and that you can find love and support elsewhere. This will help you stand up to those who may try to oppress you.

Love is the strongest tool. Therefore, surrounding yourself with those who love you unconditionally will give you the strength to tackle any challenge. Surround yourself with people who encourage you and cheer you, and celebrate your victories. As you see the results of speaking your truth and the level of attention your parents give you, set boundaries to prevent mistreatment and control. Coming from a place of love, it's important to state that any mistreatment towards you will create a greater barrier in terms of communication because nobody wants to put up with abusive language at every social gathering. We cannot take abuse lightly because our minds are more fragile than we think. Remember that you are unique and precious, and if you are surrounded by the right group of people, they will keep reminding you of this. To further reinforce your sense of self, engage in activities and routines that celebrate your uniqueness and bring you joy. Once you have established a routine of self-love by discovering who you are and what makes you happy, you will gain the strength to resist oppression. By prioritising self-love, you will attain peace, which will enable you to respond to abusive parents without resorting to aggressive or harsh language. Shouting only begets more shouting, and it only invites negativity into your life.

Love makes the world go round and keeps families united. There is love waiting for you in the world, and you can be loved. In difficult family situations, you can be the source of love and a beacon of light that others can look to. Whether you can bring your biological family together through love and compassion or whether you choose to find a new family, know that you have the power to do so. Recognise and understand the differences between your beliefs and those of your family. It's okay to have your opinions; you never know what they might lead to. Accept your family's history, and realise that it's normal to have feelings, no matter who you are. In this life, we need a family - A family that loves, supports and accepts you unconditionally is a true treasure.

Never give up on finding a family, because family is forever (WandaVision, 2021).

02. Amongst Your Friends

2.1. MAKING FRIENDS

Our friends are the next significant relationship circle we look to for support as we build our family. Our first friendships often start in infancy, depending on the social activities our parents engage in. Then, when we started going to nursery/pre-school, we were let off the leash to interact with the other children in the play area. Making friends seems effortless at this stage as we simply play in a way that feels comfortable and end up bonding with others without feeling the pressure to impress. When playing, pre-schoolers are completely themselves. However, as children enter school, there is an evolving hierarchy system where some children become the centre of attention and others are left behind. Popularity becomes a separating factor for the crowd. Making friends in such situations can be quite challenging, especially if you're trying to find a safe place amongst the cliques or be recognised and loved by the popular kids. The danger of making friends in school and life is trying to fit into a group whose beliefs don't align with yours. Deep down, we're all looking for friends, and that's perfectly fine, as we humans are social beings, and there's often societal pressure to try and fit in with others' preferences to reduce the likelihood of offending them. However, trying to impress people by presenting an image that is not true to ourselves can draw us away from authentic friendships and limits our chances of finding friends who are a perfect fit for our social circle.

Understandably, making friends is sometimes a scary process because it requires both mental and emotional effort to be successful. By disclosing our personal information to strangers who might misuse the information we provide them, we expose ourselves to vulnerability. We may feel nervous about what the other person might think of us, but we should remember that they are probably feeling the same way. They might also be anxious about what you will say to them or what they will say to impress you. It is of course wise to begin with light-hearted subjects as it's easier on the mind when communicating with a stranger. As you progress, you can gradually open up about more personal matters. When making friends, try to know how eager the other person is to engage in a conversation with you. Having a balanced conversation is crucial for forming strong friendships. Talking about yourself is important, but it's also important to listen to others and show interest in their thoughts, interests and experiences. Being open and honest about your preferences is a fantastic starting point. When both of you are open and honest, you can talk about and appreciate a variety of topics. The most authentic and long-lasting friendships are ones that are not built on lies. If you find that a particular person doesn't seem to connect with you on a deeper level, don't force the relationship or try to please them. Instead, trust that your authentic energy will attract the right individuals who you can form meaningful and fulfilling connections with.

For those who are socially shy and introverted, making new friends can be overwhelming. However, this doesn't mean that they don't desire friendship. In these situations, we need to take the initiative and create a safe space for the other person. Ask them questions and reveal your interests to see if a connection can be formed. You may be surprised to find that people who initially seem different from you may have more in common than you think (I learnt that from the 1985 film "The Breakfast Club"). Therefore, when you find the right group of friends, keep appreciating the diversity in people's personalities, backgrounds and histories. It's also okay to take a break when you don't have the energy to connect with others. When you do have the energy and are in the right mind-set, make friends with an open heart and mind. The opportunities for friendship are endless - from the cashier at the store to the student in class to the individual on the bus to the companion on your holiday. Everywhere you go in life, there is a chance to find friends who you can closely connect with.

2.2. DISCOVERING DIFFERENCES

Trying to make friends can be a fun and rewarding experience, but it's important to be mindful of the behaviour of those people who you are trying to befriend. From this, you can make wise relationship choices. Having trouble connecting with family due to differences of opinions can be challenging. However, making friends provides you with an opportunity to be your authentic self without feeling the pressure to conform to others' expectations. If you have experienced a traumatic childhood where you felt the need to constantly please your parents, building meaningful relationships with the right people can help you recognise and overcome any toxic habits you may have developed as a result.

To make friends, one must strike a balance between valuing each person's distinctive differences and seeking out something in common to connect over. When discovering the differences, observe the interaction and assess if there is mutual interest in wanting to stay connected. Do you accept each other despite the differences and look forward to seeing each other? When differences arise, it's important to avoid making insulting remarks; instead, approach each other with an open mind.

Everyone has a unique personality and views, and these differences should not dictate one's overall opinion of a person. Forming strong friendships is about having patience, not rushing to conclusions, and investing time and effort in getting to know someone gradually and deeply. The depth and intimacy of a friendship will grow over time, depending on the speed and intensity of your connection. I have personally experienced the depth of friendship that can come from embracing differences. For example, I spend most of my leisure time enjoying films, TV shows, crafting and drawing, whereas one of my close friends doesn't enjoy these activities and has her own set of interests. However, despite these differences, we engage in deep and meaningful conversations for hours.

In my experience, determining compatibility with people is challenging until you have spent enough time interacting with them and getting to know them. It takes time to analyse how many common subjects you can discuss, how many differences exist and how much effort both sides are willing to put into the friendship to keep it going. Both you and your friend will likely have differing beliefs about various aspects of life, such as sex, work, relationships, religion and law. When discussing these beliefs, it's important to express them without being insulting or offensive. The way you frame a point may make the other person feel offended, and an emotional reaction may occur. Part of staying true to yourself is being able to live out your beliefs with your friends, even if they don't agree with you completely. A true friend will accept and respect your differences as long as you do the same for them. The friendship can only be successful when both sides are able to be their authentic selves and appreciate each other's unique perspectives and personalities. When both sides can embrace their differences and appreciate the diversity they bring to the friendship, it becomes a truly fulfilling and successful relationship.

2.3. IDENTIFYING YOUR CIRCLE/TRIBE

When you think about your ideal circle of friends, how do you imagine spending time with them? What activities would you do with them to make you feel like your authentic self? What kind of support would you expect from them? What kind of happy memories would you like to create with them? It's up to you to choose friends who will make you feel confident and comfortable. Your circle of friends should serve as your second family, offering you a safe haven where you can be yourself and receive safety, comfort and recognition.

To determine if someone is part of your circle of friends, observe how they treat you and if their actions align with their words. Do they truly mean what they say, or do they just say something like, "I will always be there for you" and then disappear when you find yourself in a huge emotional spiral? When you express your emotions, do they impose their beliefs on you, or do they acknowledge your emotions and provide you with the love and support you need? The worst friends are those who never pay attention to your emotions and always talk about their own emotions. When communicating with your friends, do you feel like you can share your deepest and most intimate thoughts without the fear of being judged? Your true friends will not judge you but will take their time to hear you, be patient with you and will always be ready to listen to you.

Your circle of friends is not only a source of emotional support, but also a group with whom you can share life's milestones and celebrate each other's successes. Your tribe should embody the lyrics of the popular American sitcom's theme song:

> So, no one told you life was gonna be this way
> Your job's a joke, you're broke
> Your love life's D.O.A.
> It's like you're always stuck in second gear
> When it hasn't been your day, your week,
> your month
> Or even your year, but
> I'll be there for you
> (The Rembrandts, 1995)

They are there for you through thick and thin and will never diminish the value of your accomplishments or try to steal the spotlight. Instead, they will offer recognition and support, displaying their genuine interest in your life and growth. Someone who immediately draws away attention from your achievements is the last person you need in your life. They could make you feel like your achievements aren't worth celebrating. Remember that your emotions and achievements are valid and deserving of recognition, and don't let anyone undermine your emotions and achievements.

2.4. A TWO-WAY STREET

Effective communication is the key to forming and maintaining any friendship or relationship. Both parties need to put in the effort, even though it may not always be equal.

To initiate a friendship, one party must take the first step and reach out to the other. When making a new friend, don't be afraid to initiate the conversation, even if talking to a stranger feels uncomfortable. Each first interaction is a leap of faith worth taking. If you feel like you won't connect with the person or their first impression is not to your liking, you can move on. However, if you do find someone you're encouraged to befriend (you both have similar habits or express the same interests or feel a warm vibe), clear your mind of any worries and approach the situation with a mind-set like that of a baby, where you are not worried about what might go wrong. Babies approach new situations with fearlessness, not concerned with potential harm or failure. They simply take action. With this carefree mind-set, approach new opportunities for friendship confidently. Be courteous and respectful, and most importantly, stay true to yourself. Honesty about your preferred method of communication (calls, messages or meeting in person communication) can help ensure a smooth interaction.

Over time, observe how often the friend communicates with you. There are some friends with whom you may not communicate regularly, but whenever you do, it's as if no time has passed. These types of friendships are especially valuable as both parties prioritise the relationship, making the time and effort to stay connected despite the busy schedules. However, some friends require regular and consistent interaction (weekly or even daily). Having regular communication helps foster a deeper understanding and connection between friends. It allows for a more open exchange of ideas and experiences, which could potentially lead to a deeper, more meaningful relationship. Despite geographical barriers, technology has made it possible for people to form meaningful relationships even from afar. In fact, the rise of technology has given birth to the concept of "online friends" or "internet friends", where people can connect and build relationships through games, social media and other digital platforms.

However, if you notice an imbalance in communication, take care of the situation and yourself. Take care of the situation by being open and honest with the person about how you feel regarding the dynamic. If you feel that there is an imbalance in the effort put into the friendship, it's okay to communicate this. The best way to express your opinion is by using sentences that start with "I feel that...". By using these words, you eliminate the possibility of using labels against the other person, and you still get to voice your concerns. If a person respects you, they will be willing to listen to you and work towards finding a solution that is fair for both parties. If the person is unwilling to listen, it's important to prioritise your own well-being by creating distance between yourself and the person. This will allow you to acknowledge and validate your own feelings. Treat yourself to something that brings you joy, or try consider confiding in a trusted person about the situation. Some friends might suddenly stop interacting as much as they used to, and there could be several reasons for this. One possibility is that they are struggling because of personal challenges and need time to process their emotions. Once they get comfortable, they'll eventually open up and share with you. However, if you find yourself always initiating contact and rarely receiving a response, you may start to feel mentally exhausted. If you especially observe that they are active on social media and interacting with others, but ignoring your messages, it may indicate a lack of interest in maintaining the friendship. In such cases, it's best to step back; see if they make any effort to reach out to you. A healthy friendship requires effort from both parties, and it's only fair to expect mutual effort in maintaining the relationship.

2.5. BEHAVIOUR IN YOUR SOCIAL CIRCLE

As your friend circle should be a safe place for you to express yourself, there's some sort of expectation of how our friends should treat us, especially if you all profess to be friends who support one another through thick and thin. Take a moment to reflect on what your ideal friendship circle would look like - would you like to receive validation for your feelings, recognition for your accomplishments and comfort in both good and bad times? These are all essential elements of human connection, and they should be present in any meaningful friendship.

All of us have the right to express our feelings, as long as they're not aggressive or disrespectful towards others. The right friend circle will listen and acknowledge these feelings, allowing us to support each other through our emotions. A famous proverb goes like this: "A problem shared is a problem halved". It implies that when we share our struggles and experiences, it can ease the burden and make us feel validated. Expressing our feelings should be done without fear of judgement, as being judged can invalidate our emotions and amplify our sadness. Finding a space where our feelings are accepted and understood is crucial for our emotional well-being. However, if your friends are insulting your feelings, it may be a sign of toxic behaviour and should not be ignored. The response you receive from your friends when you open up to them and express your emotions when they are around should demonstrate the true measure of a strong friendship. Allowing your friends to continually insult you only perpetuates the behaviour and allows them to continue mistreating you without them realising the harm they're causing. In these cases, it's important to stand up for yourself and communicate the negative impact of their actions towards you.

If they continue to dismiss your feelings, it is necessary to reduce your emotional investment in the friendship regardless of how often your brain tells you that they might change later. A genuine friend circle will be eager to understand who you are as a person, from your most important beliefs to your unique quirks. This kind of interest and attention indicates a deep level of care and concern. Whether it's the way you approach a task or the way you eat your meals, a good friend will seek to understand all aspects of your life. This level of understanding helps them provide the right kind of support, as they'll be able to recognise what causes different emotional responses in you and respond accordingly.

Humility is a valuable trait that demonstrates a genuine concern for others before oneself. In today's fast-paced world, it can be difficult to find people who embody this quality - someone who willingly puts others' happiness above their desires and wants displays pure humility. It's the act of putting someone else's happiness before your own and sacrificing what you may want for their sake. This selfless attitude is a true display of love and one that can be seen in acts of heroism such as sacrificing one's life for a friend (The Bible - John 15:13). In everyday life, humility can be shown in simple gestures, such as holding a door open for someone, letting someone have the last sweet treat, admitting our mistakes and recognising when humility is being displayed and responding in the same manner. When someone is humble enough to apologise for their mistakes, we should always strive to recognise and respond in humility with kindness and appreciation, rather than pass judgement. I prefer to live by the following quote, which I'll never forget:

I don't judge people on their worst mistakes.
(Avengers Endgame, 2019)

Celebrating life's milestones and achievements with close friends is a meaningful and uplifting experience. These moments of recognition and support can provide the encouragement and confidence to continue striving for success. On the other hand, during times of adversity, it's important to have friends who offer comfort and understanding. Such a supportive friend circle can make a significant difference in maintaining one's self-esteem and providing the love and validation needed to overcome challenges. If you feel like you're not receiving the level of support and celebration you need from your friends, it may be worth re-evaluating your friendships and finding a group that truly supports and celebrates your journey through life.

2.6. JOURNEY THROUGH LIFE: NAVIGATING RELATIONSHIPS AND SAYING GOODBYE

The quote "Life is a journey" is true, no doubt. This quote perfectly embodies the constant progression and growth that we experience as we move forward in life. We grow in knowledge, skills and perspectives as we face new challenges and opportunities, some of which may even take us to different parts of the world. The journey is ongoing and holds endless possibilities for personal development. Family and friends are an integral part of our lives, but over time, certain circumstances may lead us to say goodbye to some of them.

This can happen for various reasons, such as a new job, relocating closer to family or the start of a new romantic relationship. If you've had a similar experience as I have, you may have had to bid farewell to friends from school or the local community when you had to move across the country with your parents for a new job opportunity. Saying goodbye to close friends with whom you've formed a strong bond can be very difficult. You may find yourself wondering when you will see each other again, whether you'll remain in contact, if your shared memories will endure over time and if you both will have fun the same way again. The journey of life can be daunting, especially when we lose friends along the way, as we are all looking for a place of love in our lives. Despite this, we should view it as our life's journey towards love and relationships. Maintaining strong connections with friends despite life's changes is a true testament to the depth of a friendship. When two individuals make an effort to stay in touch, it highlights the intimacy and mutual affection they share. These friendships are truly precious and worth cherishing.

At times, the communication between friends may slowly fade as life goes on. This can happen due to a variety of reasons such as changes in personal growth leading to differences in the relationship, shifting focus to other priorities or relationships and a lack of compatibility that prompts the search for new friends. Some of those reasons for fading friendships can be heartbreaking, especially when they are due to unintentional miscommunication or misunderstanding. Despite our best efforts to communicate honestly and respectfully, there may be instances where our friends misunderstand us and distance themselves from us. This can be especially painful when it occurs without any intention to cause harm. I can personally relate to this, as I share this experience. This can be disheartening when you question what you did wrong and what caused the sudden change in the person's perception. It's natural to try to repair the relationship by explaining your side of the story, but sometimes, no matter how much effort you put in, the other side may still choose to walk away. In such cases, it's important to remember that a friendship requires effort and understanding from both parties. If only one person is willing to work on it, it becomes more of a pursuit than a true friendship.

As friends spend time together and create memories, strong emotional bonds can form within the relationship, making it difficult to let go. I speak from experience when I say that this can be a difficult process. It's important to recognise that a friendship should come with mutual understanding and respect. If someone is not treating you in a way that aligns with these values, it may be worth considering if the friendship is worth maintaining. Before making a decision, ask yourself why you still want to be around this person despite their mistreatment towards you. Then ask yourself if it is worth the cost of your mental and emotional well-being. Chasing after individuals who do not give you the respect and understanding you deserve, while neglecting those who actively strive to treat you well, is a common trap that many people fall into. We can become so focused and attached to the people we desire in our lives, that we often overlook those who truly care about us. By expanding our understanding of what and who we truly need in our lives, we can bring in positive and supportive individuals while letting go of those who harm us.

You can have the loving relationships you've always dreamed of only if you are willing to acknowledge the abuse you're experiencing from toxic people and walk away from them. By doing so you free up space in your life for people who are worth your time and effort. This will allow you to form meaningful connections with the right people. As you journey through life, you come to understand that some people are only meant to be in your life for a certain chapter.

When that chapter comes to an end, we part ways peacefully and continue growing and moving forward with our respective lives. Saying goodbye to these individuals doesn't have to be a negative experience. By choosing to view it as a peaceful departure, rather than a loss, we can focus on the growth and opportunities that come with new beginnings. What's great about friends is that they can impart knowledge that will be useful to us in the future. As we mature and face new challenges, the memories and wisdom we shared with our friends serve as a reminder of the positive impact they have had on our lives. It's important to remember that personal growth often leads to changes in our personalities, and that's okay. There's always room for self-improvement and growth, much like how trees continue to grow taller and stronger.

As we mature, we may become less relatable to one person and more relatable to another. Therefore, we never really lose friends, but rather our relationships may take on new forms or become more meaningful with different individuals as we continue to grow. Sometimes a friend may be there for a specific reason or season in our lives, and as we grow, our paths may diverge. On the other hand, some friendships may endure for many years to come.

2.7. LOGICALLY ANALYSE YOUR FRIEND CIRCLE

Regularly analysing your friend circle is a good practice that everyone should adopt. It's important to take a critical and thoughtful look at the dynamics of your friendships. Analyse the way people treat you, reflect on how those actions make you feel and make a deliberate decision on what steps to take based on your feelings. Logic should play a significant role in this process. For example, a true friend who loves you would exhibit qualities like compassion, kindness, care and all other positive traits that define someone who treats you with respect and love. A toxic person is someone who causes harm to your mental, physical and emotional well-being and lacks respect towards your values and identity. Listen to what your mind and body are communicating to you. Do you feel discomfort when you're around certain people? Do you feel like you can't be yourself with them? Do you feel like you have to put on an act to impress them or feel accepted? If you said yes to all these questions, it's a sign that they may not be the right friends for you. The right friends will embrace and accept you for who you are, without any expectations or conditions. They will appreciate and support the unique, authentic person that you are, no matter how crazy or weird you might think you are.

To make friends, be yourself and respect others' boundaries, even if there are differences. A true friend respects others' boundaries, attends to their needs, supports them and loves them as they are. This is how friendships are formed. I always remember the following quote from Disney when making friends:

To make a friend, you need to be a friend.
(Lilo and Stitch: The Series, S1 E8 "Yapper" 2003)

By logically analysing your friendships based on their ability to provide the type of support you need, the way you want to receive love and how valued they make you feel, you can create a circle of genuine love that will empower you to navigate life's challenges. Everybody has a different method of receiving love. A book called "The 5 Love Languages" by Gary Chapman will help you explore your own preferences. Part of cultivating strong friendships is understanding and respecting each other's preferred methods of showing and receiving love. We may not always instinctively know how to best support our friends. However, open communication and a willingness to learn can go a long way in making sure that our loved ones feel loved. It's okay to ask for clarification or share our own needs. No one can accurately "read" another person like an open book, especially if that person has not made their feelings and needs clear.

By sharing our love and life experiences, we can cultivate the type of love we desire for ourselves and others. Life is a crazy journey, and surrounding ourselves with people who care about us ensures that we don't have to undertake the journey alone. As previously stated, humans are social creatures by nature, and lack of social support and loneliness can have negative impacts on both mental and physical health, including increased risk of depression and cardiovascular disease and weakened immune system. Therefore, surround yourself with loving friends who you can reach out to without thinking twice about. Refrain from suffering in silence and allow the right friends to help you heal and uplift you in wonderful ways. The right friends will love you exactly as you are. As a famous quote from an American sitcom says:

Life is unpredictable. Not everything is in our control, but as long as we're with the right people, we can handle anything.

(Brooklyn Nine-Nine, S5 E22 "Jake & Amy" 2018)

03. At Your Workplace

3.1. SCHOOL AND EDUCATION

We are all required to go to school to educate ourselves. This is the first stage of learning for our future professional careers. Since this is when a young child begins to experience life outside of the home, the school environment is always extremely frightening at first. You begin to meet other people your age, and this is when you start forming relationships. Of course, at such a young age, no one knows how to do it, but it's interesting to note that children don't worry or think about how to impress others or how to present their best selves. A heart-warming moment is when two young children first encounter each other and engage in spontaneous, playful and carefree interaction, simply by being their authentic selves. Imagine a world, where all of us, including adults, could be ourselves and play together, without worrying about what others might think of us or having to hide anything. The wonderful thing about children is that they are unaware of concepts like popularity or first-impressions. Children's innocence allows them to form connections without prejudices, as they have not yet learned to judge others based on social norms and biases. It is devastating when children are influenced to conform to societal norms and biases, limiting their natural ability to form relationships based on genuine connection. What goes unnoticed over time is that as children go through school, they develop their unique perceptions of the world. These perceptions largely depend on what they've been taught by their everyday surroundings. They primarily learn from their parents, as they depend on them the most. The second group of people they learn from the most is their friends.

Therefore, it's important for parents to teach their children that they should be authentic when making friends. I am aware that everyone wants to be popular - to be recognised, admired and valued by the world. Deep down, we all want to be overwhelmed with love, but if we have to sacrifice the good parts of ourselves to obtain it, it will never be satisfying. Not everyone realises that what we truly want is to be loved for what we are and not for what the world wants us to be.

From kindergarten to university, you'll likely make and lose many friends. Maintaining one's individuality and surrounding oneself with supportive individuals is essential for a successful school experience. Cady Heron from "Mean Girls" (2004) is a perfect example of what happens when you pretend to be someone you're not, to fit in a group. The last thing you want to happen is to end up like Cady Heron, who lost her authenticity by joining the popular clique, leading to her true friends' rejection and her eventual alienation.

3.2. ENTERING THE WORKPLACE

Entering the workforce for the first time can be a daunting experience. Just like starting school, it can be scary to be thrown into a new environment with a diverse group of people who are all working together towards a common goal. At work, not only is it important to make a positive professional impression through your work performance, but it is also important to create a welcoming and approachable personal impression to facilitate easier interactions with colleagues.

While not all professional relationships can be perfect, it's important to make an effort to be friendly. Personal interactions with your team are just as important as professional interactions. Despite the professional standards that need to be met, it's important to remember that we're all still human and have emotions and need support. Hopefully, when starting in a new workplace, you will be able to get a sense of the work culture and dynamics of how people interact and collaborate. Working as part of a team requires following the company's values and working within the established dynamics to be a good fit. However, it's also important to maintain your individuality and stay true to who you are. You are not a machine programmed to follow the same code as others, but a unique individual who has the potential to either shine as a valued colleague or develop a negative reputation based on your actions and behaviour. When interacting with colleagues for the first time, it's always good to be open to getting to know them, even if there's a risk of vulnerability.

Not everyone may get along well with you, but by being honest, you can better understand the boundaries of being yourself in the workplace. Age, background and other differences should not be a barrier to developing connections with colleagues. In fact, people who appear to be the most different from us can have more in common with us. Some colleagues may be instantly drawn to your positive energy and friendly demeanour, leading to light-hearted and enjoyable interactions. In some cases, these positive relationships between colleagues can develop into personal friendships outside the workplace, with both parties putting in the effort to maintain the connection. Having supportive friends in and outside of work can contribute to your overall happiness and well-being.

Building relationships within and across departments can make you a valuable resource and connect you with colleagues who share similar interests and values. For introverts, the thought of interacting with others may cause some nervousness. That's okay, and it's a common experience for many people. However, opportunities for building relationships may arise when you are assigned tasks that require inter-departmental collaboration. Sometimes, even if you try your hardest, you may face rejection or insults from colleagues. In these cases, it's important to ignore the insults and not take them personally. However, if the behaviour becomes disrespectful, insulting or hurtful, it goes against the universal work ethic of non-discrimination. This type of behaviour creates a hostile work environment and makes a person lose interest in the job.

3.3. EXPERIENCING CONTINUOUS MISTREATMENT FROM COLLEAGUES

No one wants to face mistreatment in their workplace and it is equally important to feel comfortable and confident in expressing one's self. As a human being, you deserve to be treated with respect and dignity. So, if you find yourself in a situation where you're being mistreated, it's important to ask yourself why you're tolerating it. Why should you endure such mistreatment? You are just as worthy and deserving of respect as anyone else.

To avoid drama in the workplace, some people refrain from engaging in confrontations. However, the reality is that the drama is already at a high level with the person criticising you, leading to a significant amount of stress. In my experience, confronting the person and addressing the issue head-on is often the most sensible way to deal with a conflict. It's important to let them know that their behaviour is not acceptable. If they don't listen to your concerns, don't hesitate to escalate the issue to someone in a higher position, such as human resources person, a supervisor or a trusted colleague.

The right workplace should prioritise resolving conflicts to ensure a harmonious work environment for all employees. Any organisation will undoubtedly have some sort of code of conduct or standard stating that discrimination and abuse will not be accepted there (I can't think of a single workplace that doesn't have a code of conduct or ethic that addresses this). Conflicts amongst colleagues adversely affect the smooth operation of tasks in the workplace. When considering cooperation within a business, I always keep in mind the following phrase from a Pixar film:

A company is like an enormous clock. It only works if all the little cogs mesh together.

(The Incredibles, 2004)

Our work-life is crucial as it enables us to earn a living and support ourselves and our loved ones. It's essential to maintain a positive attitude and not let negative comments or behaviour from colleagues affect us deeply. Additionally, seeking new opportunities and changing our work environment can also greatly improve our overall experience and satisfaction in the workplace. Given the substantial amount of time we spend at work each week, it's crucial to prioritise our mental and emotional well-being while on the job. Our mental health is not as robust as we believe it to be. It's sensitive and vulnerable and needs to be taken care of if we want to perform to the best of our ability. Having a supportive, organised and cooperative team is of utmost importance in any workplace. In a team environment, we may still be ourselves because we each have strengths that the team may lack. Don't be afraid to be yourself because you have something unique to offer and can contribute to completing a task by offering a different approach or perspective. Our ideas may be rejected, but that doesn't mean that we should stop expressing them. There is someone out there who will appreciate them. Even if it's just a fragment of an idea, your contribution can still be incredibly helpful to the team in organising and structuring a final concept. On some occasions, your input can bring fresh perspectives and valuable insights, making a positive impact on the team's end result. So, don't underestimate the power of your involvement; every little bit counts.

If no one in the workplace values you, I hope that you can change jobs if you can. There will be a place in this world where you will be accepted and appreciated for who you are. As I share this, I want to acknowledge that there are unfortunate cases, where people have struggled to create the work environment they desire because of responsibilities like taking care of family members or paying bills. However, I hope that whichever situation you find yourself in, you can get the support you need because no one should suffer in silence. When people collaborate, they can accomplish so much more. They don't have to agree with each other on everything, but they can learn to appreciate and accept each other's differences to achieve a common goal. As once said by John C. Maxwell, teamwork makes the dream work.

3.4. WHAT'S YOUR PASSION?

Your job provides the opportunity for you to be a professional in your field of choice. If you could choose any profession, what would it be? Remember, work should be fulfilling and enjoyable, not a chore. Embrace your career with enthusiasm and let it be a platform for you to be whoever you aspire to be. It's certainly a scary world out there, especially when we have to put ourselves out there and risk rejection. Despite this fear, it's important to remember that success comes from not giving up. If your current employers are not recognising the unique skills and contributions you bring to the table, it may indicate that the job is not aligned with your strengths and expertise. This could serve as a hint that a more suitable and fulfilling opportunity may exist for you.

Combining your interests and passions with your profession can be a powerful way to find fulfilment in both your personal and professional lives. For example, in my early teenage years, I found joy and peace in building Airfix plastic model kits. These models helped me develop an ever-expanding appreciation for the operation of vehicles. Over time, I became increasingly drawn to visualising aircraft and knew that I wanted to pursue a career in this field.

Therefore, I carefully evaluated potential career options and decided to pursue a suitable degree. The journey was challenging, but I gained valuable work experience and was willing to move across the country multiple times. Now, my hard work has paid off, and I am proud to work as an engineer in the aircraft industry. I found my calling, and I know that you can too. The following is a quote that I carry with me everywhere I go:

If you put your mind to it,
you can accomplish anything.
(Back to the Future, 1985)

Your passions can change over time, but that doesn't mean that any part of your life was wasted in the wrong career. Every job can serve as a stepping stone that can help you discover your true calling. Make the most of your work, and take pleasure in what you do, for you do it to support your family and yourself. There will inevitably be aspects of work that are not enjoyable or cause stress because everyone experiences stress in their work-life to some extent. It's important to keep a positive outlook and not let stress from work impact your well-being.

A supportive team can help fuel your passions and drive you to achieve your goals. Falling into a cycle of feeling trapped in your job and constantly complaining about it can harm your mental health. Follow your passions, and if you find something you enjoy, don't give it up. Pursuing your passions can inspire you to do the impossible.

3.5. HANDLING STRESS IN THE WORKPLACE

There are several methods to deal with stress that occurs in the workplace. Some of them are:

- Stay put until the storm passes;
- Speak up about the stress, and get help;
- Change the situation;

These methods can be helpful to some extent. However, a well-thought-out strategy can give you the confidence to know that you have done everything in your power to handle the situation. By taking a proactive approach, you can say with certainty, "I did my best, and I couldn't have done any better".

Stress in the workplace is unavoidable, but it's how we handle it that ultimately defines our strength and success. If you choose to follow any of the three options mentioned above, during a period of workplace stress, such as a challenging project or tight deadline, it's important to remember that it's only temporary and keep pushing forward to achieve the goal. This fosters perseverance and showcases our ability to overcome difficulties and succeed. Teamwork is also crucial during these times, as it provides support and helps everyone reach the target together.

If you're experiencing high levels of stress that you've been unable to manage for an extended period of time, I recommend taking action to address it. Prolonged stress can cause a lot of mental and emotional harm. You may not be able to work to the best of your ability; your temper may be affected, making you more prone to emotional outbursts or you may start to suffer from illnesses. Don't suffer in silence. Take a step back and examine the situation. It's crucial to understand your limits and know when you're taking on more than you can handle. Trying to pretend you're capable of handling everything only leads to increased levels of stress for you, and you could pass the stress onto others as well. Know your limitations; otherwise, you can't work to the best of your ability, can you? If you find yourself overwhelmed with your work, don't be afraid to bring it to the attention of your team or supervisor. Teams are meant to help each other out and distribute workload evenly. It's possible that someone on the team may have a lighter workload and can offer to help. By openly addressing the issue, you'll create a better balance and be better equipped to handle the stress and succeed in your career. Having a supportive team will help you tackle all the challenges in your career.

If you are dealing with a huge workload and are being mistreated by co-workers, you may need to take more drastic measures. It's not the ideal work-life scenario; in fact, it's the worst. If you've tried reaching out for help and the situation doesn't improve, it may be time to consider quitting the job. Why should you sacrifice your happiness and mental health to please others? The desire to make others happy should make you happy. However, if the people around you can't be content in their surroundings, they'll eventually bring you down. Explore alternative job opportunities that can provide a more cooperative and respectable work environment. You can quietly search for a new job and then resign, or if you're feeling bold, resign immediately and actively search for the next job opportunity.

3.6. LONG-TERM CAREER PLAN

It's always good to have a plan for your career goals, but sometimes even a well-defined goal can lead you down a different career path. In either case, you discover what you want to do. There won't be much fulfilment if you follow people's advice blindly or have a job only for the sake of working; instead, you risk having a job that you continually complain about. However, this doesn't mean we should join in with the complaining simply because it's a common subject. Constantly complaining about our jobs without actually taking action to make the situation better will drain you and everyone around you. Be honest about what you enjoy or are passionate about in your job, and make sure to express it. We have the freedom to do whatever we want to do and be whoever we want to be. However, to work towards that goal of our dream job or career, we need a plan. Miracles don't just happen; we need to work towards them.

To find a fulfilling career, start by identifying your passions and unique talents. Take time to reflect; search for opportunities that align with your interests. You can utilise the internet and seek advice from friends to create a list of potential career options. Consider each option carefully, and choose the option that aligns with your values and goals. Having a strategic approach to finding your ideal career is perfectly acceptable; after all, you want to be content with your career until the day you retire and can finally give yourself a pat on the back and say, "Good job!". Having a career you love can make you feel good about yourself, which you can then share with others to motivate them.

While finding a job that you enjoy is a great accomplishment, it's important to remember that work is a means to an end, not the end itself. Our primary reason for working is to earn a livelihood, so we can support ourselves and live a fulfilling life. However, it's equally important to prioritise personal time for ourselves. Finding a healthy balance between work and leisure is the key to leading a fulfilling life, especially if you have a family to care for. The last thing a family needs is the absence of a family member for long periods. This can negatively impact the family dynamic making the family feel as though they were never around. Children require their parents to nurture them as well as provide for them materially and emotionally. To be good parents and individuals, we need to recognise that we are not just machines designed to work tirelessly, but complex individuals with multiple facets of our identity that we can offer to the world. Make sure to prioritise rest so that you can work as effectively as possible. Remember; work hard, play hard!

The best advice that I can offer is that you seek out your passions, and find a career that aligns with them. By pursuing a career that satisfies your interests, you will be able to be yourself. Your job should not define your entire identity and purpose in life; it should be a means to support your well-being and enjoyment of life. It's okay if your passions change over time, the future is full of opportunities waiting for you to grasp. To build a fulfilling future, it takes confidence and determination to take those steps towards realising your potential. A final quote to set you off:

Your future hasn't been written yet.
No one's has. Your future is whatever you make it.
So, make it a good one!
(Back to the Future Part III, 1990)

So, go ahead, take control and make your future the best it can be.

04. Within Society

4.1. WHAT SOCIETY LOOKS LIKE?

If you were to sum up what society values the most, what would your answer be? It would be admiration, success, popularity, financial stability and an attractive partner. I'm sure we want at least one of these things.

It appears that society, as depicted through social media, values material wealth, appearance and popularity. This is evidenced by the constant representation of luxury lifestyles, fashionable clothing, flashy cars, exotic destinations and attractive women. Social media and the internet constantly present us with new, attractive things that we crave for. Additionally, the emphasis on having a high number of social media followers suggests that people desire to be well-liked and admired. People often seek out content that provides excitement and stimulation, including sexually suggestive material online. This type of consumption can harm their well-being. In pursuit of an adrenaline rush, some individuals engage in high-risk activities like partying, drug use, alcohol consumption, gambling and others. However, there are many other ways to live that don't solely depend on emotional stimulation. In certain organisations, including religious institutions, the purpose of creating a space for expression and freedom can sometimes be overshadowed by leaders who focus on maintaining order and exerting control over every detail. Despite the limitations in their control, leaders are still faced with calls for privacy invasion and demands about appropriate actions. However, not every detail can be controlled by them. I've personally encountered this issue in some organisations, where constant monitoring of actions creates a feeling of discomfort and inhibitions, making it difficult to be one's authentic self. To summarise the points discussed, it could be characterised as a culture that prioritises materialism and legalism. Materialism is when people keep buying a lot of things, whereas legalism is when there is strict adherence to the law leading to more control than freedom.

Society often places high value on the idea of having a family and owning a beautiful home, for they provide a sense of security and status. However, it's important to examine the motivations behind this desire. Is it driven by a genuine need for love and connection with others, or is it motivated by pride and a desire to impress others? When getting to know a family, did you observe mutual respect and love amongst family members, or did you see one member trying to get all the attention? In many cases, families can be torn apart by conflicts, abuse and divorce, which raises questions about the true nature of the relationships within the family. People's opinions and preferences, whether expressed through words or actions, can often be misleading. Pay close attention to what people say as well as what they do, since their actions will reveal their true intentions.

The saying "actions speak louder than words" is particularly relevant in this context, as it highlights the importance of observing a person's behaviour to gain insight into their character. To navigate the complexities of society, it's essential to keep a close eye on people's behaviour. Keep an eye out for any red flags or words that don't match actions. Trusting your intuition takes courage, especially in a world where many people try to undermine it. Differentiating between your intuition and a misleading thought is key to making informed decisions. Your intuition is meant to guide you down a safe path, and usually, there is an absence of fear accompanying it. However, if a thought is accompanied by deep-seated fear, it may be time to reflect on where this fear is coming from. This fear could stem from someone else's belief, a traumatic experience or an idea imposed on you subconsciously. In this case, recognising the source of the fear is crucial in eliminating misleading thoughts that may hold you back from opportunities for growth.

A personal example I'd like to share with you is that when I was growing up, I was heavily disciplined to do household chores to the highest standards. No matter how many times I did my job to the best of my ability, I was always told where I went wrong, and I barely received any praise for the good work I had done. Along with a list of wrongdoings that was given to me, I was subjected to an aggressive voice that kept telling me that I wasn't performing up to the mark. Over time, I convinced myself that I was incapable of performing a job well and that my past mistakes rendered me incompetent for good jobs. My confidence decreased, and I found myself volunteering less for tasks. I even began punishing myself if I felt that my work wasn't good enough. I even started to think that I wouldn't stand a chance when trying new things. Joining the Empath Academy, I learned some comforting truths, such as: everyone makes mistakes, we can't be perfect because we're only human, you can always try again, and you can only do your best. Meditating on these truths, I started to believe that I was capable of achieving more. The voice in my head that once told me I wasn't good enough has transformed into a belief that I can do anything I desire. This experience allowed me to develop a growth mindset, where I became more willing to help others and confident in my abilities to achieve anything I set my mind to. I also learned that making mistakes is a natural part of the learning process and that there are always opportunities to learn from them and make things right.

Social media can offer insights into the popular desires of society, but it can also reinforce a conformist mentality by promoting trends and encouraging people to conform to certain standards and expectations. Individuals with differing views are often harshly judged and ostracised. Those who prioritise humility, reduced consumption and putting others first are becoming rare in our society. Our society seems to prioritise what we can gain rather than what we can contribute. The focus is on winning rather than working together to reach a common goal. Despite centuries of progress, issues such as racism, sexism, war, harassment and theft continue to persist. This shows that there hasn't been any real progress made in tackling these problems. The monotonous routine of "eat, sleep, work, repeat" is driven by a desire for security and the fear of losing it. The notion of family security is also tied to this, as we often feel the need to showcase a successful partner or children as a symbol of our achievements.

4.2. WHAT YOU BELIEVE

Societal norms can influence what is perceived as normal and valuable, but it's crucial to reflect on and prioritise your own beliefs and values. It can be tempting to conform to societal expectations, such as having sex early in life, being married and owning a house or car by a certain age, but not everyone fits into these moulds. Some people may choose to focus on other priorities, like volunteering, caring for a sick family member or taking time to discover their true desires. It's crucial to remain true to your own beliefs, even if they differ from society's norms. Making important life decisions due to societal pressure without carefully weighing the consequences can lead to disastrous effects.

There can also be misdirection on what truths to believe. There are people who experience intense emotions in certain situations, leading them to believe that their feelings are an accurate reflection of reality. However, truth cannot be based on emotions. The concept of truth requires thorough investigation in life, rather than blindly accepting it just because it is a popular belief. We may not always know the truth immediately in all situations, but we can explore it by considering all aspects and asking questions. Instead of blindly following trends, take the time to understand who you are, what your values and passions are and what you truly want in life. Don't let outside influences from family and friends cloud your judgement. Embrace your unique perspectives and ideas, even if they differ from what society deems normal. Happiness should come from within, not from external validation. Relying on society's praise for happiness can lead to emotional turmoil and even physical illnesses. Have you ever had an idea or thought that you wanted to express, but were prevented from doing so by someone else?

To be able to express our true selves, it is important to find people who are willing to listen to us and respect our beliefs. This can be a challenging step, as it requires vulnerability, but by gradually sharing parts of ourselves, we can assess how much others respect us. If we encounter red flags and feel uncomfortable, it is important to take action and step back. We may have had many wonderful ideas in life that went unheard, but finding a supportive friend circle allows us to be noticed for who we are rather than what others expect us to be.

The following quote from a Disney film introduces the next section:

> *Did you ever feel like there was a whole other person inside you just looking for a way to come out?*
>
> *(High School Musical, 2006)*

4.3. WHEN DISAGREEMENTS ARISE

Disagreements between people are an inevitable aspect of diversity. They don't have to be negative, but rather a reflection of different approaches to a particular subject. The important thing is how we handle these differences. Do we become hostile and feel a need to prove ourselves right, or do we acknowledge and value the other person's viewpoint? It's up to us to determine how we deal with such situations. A wise person understands that having different opinions is acceptable. Though we all live in the same world, our perceptions of it are unique. We have the power to shape our perception, but not those of others. Trying to change someone else's perspective is like trying to fit a square peg into a round hole. When facing differences, it's important to take into account both our reaction and the reaction of the other person. The most important thing is not to overreact by shouting or degrading someone's views when encountering a different perspective. It's understandable that when faced with a differing opinion, you may feel the urge to interrupt and convince the other person to see things from your perspective. However, it's important to listen and respect their viewpoint first before expressing your own. Disagreements don't have to be negative, and it's possible to respectfully disagree with someone who holds a different opinion. It's also important to keep in mind that people will always have different perspectives, and part of accepting others is accepting them for who they are, not trying to change them. While it's possible to offer new perspectives, ultimately it's up to the individual to decide what they believe. So, instead of trying to completely change their mind, focus on presenting different viewpoints and allowing them to come to their own conclusions.

When facing disagreement with another person's opinion, it's common to feel as though your own opinions are not being acknowledged or respected. This is a normal reaction, but it's important to keep in mind that your opinions hold just as much value, regardless of whether others agree with them or not. It's important to remember that valid opinions are those that are respectful and considerate of others. While it can be tempting to argue and try to prove your point, it's often more productive to have a respectful dialogue and be open to hearing each other out. If the other person becomes overly aggressive or refuses to listen, you have the right to end the conversation. It's important to remember that everyone deserves to be respected in a conversation, regardless of their opinions. In a society, people will have different opinions. However, it's essential to maintain your own opinions without succumbing to external influences.

4.4. A SCARY PLACE

People have different approaches to life and often find comfort in what is familiar to them. While some people seek adventure and travel to far-off places to seek answers or fight for a cause, others might choose to stay within the boundaries of their hometown and never leave it. Both approaches are perfectly valid, and each person's experiences and insights are shaped by the choices they make. The world is full of the unknown, and exploring it can be scary, especially for the young and impressionable. The media and news frequently promote fear, which can discourage people from exploring and experiencing the world. However, those who do travel are likely to gain a deeper understanding and appreciation of the world we live in.

A tough pill to swallow is the reality that we cannot spend our entire lives avoiding discomfort and fear. We all experience discomfort in various situations, whether it be in social situations, the workplace, our homes, or any place in the world we will travel to. Our darkest secrets being revealed and the uncertainty of how we'll be perceived for them are two prevalent fears. While some may have to confess to wrongdoing or a crime, there are others whose fear is so deeply ingrained that they will go to great lengths to hide the truth.

Fear is deeply ingrained in many individuals and permeates various areas of the world. Living with constant fear can lead to the belief that the world is a dangerous place and that one must always be cautious. Fear is a more powerful force than we realise and can unconsciously drive us to commit harmful acts and cause immense pain to others and ourselves. When fear takes hold, it can lead to the loss of one's identity and even their sanity.

In life, we always have a choice. We can either let fear control us or we can step forward with courage and defy the limiting beliefs in our minds. Although it's natural to feel scared, especially when we don't have control of the situation, it's important to remember that there will be many situations in life where we won't have complete control, no matter how hard we try. Then, our best course of action will be to handle each situation to the best of our ability and maintain a positive perspective even if things don't go according to our plans. Sometimes our biggest challenges and moments of weakness are opportunities for growth and not defeat. Despite what others might say, we always have the power to learn and grow from our experiences. To overcome fear, it's crucial to fill our hearts with love. Love and fear cannot coexist, as love will always drive out fear. This is emphasised in the Bible, where 1 John 4:18 states, "There is no fear in love, for perfect love casts out fear".

4.5. OVERCOMING SOCIETAL PRESSURE AND FEAR

So, what will you do when faced with people trying to control how you should live your life? Will you give in to societal expectations or stand firm in your beliefs and values? It's easier said than done. However, there are certain steps you can take to remain true to yourself and not be swayed by society's pressures. Society will often use fear as a tool to get you to conform to their image of you.

From personal experience, trying to conform to the perception of others can lead to unhappiness and the suppression of one's true self. This may lead to unhealthy behaviour and habits. To combat this, it's important to surround yourself with genuine friends and family who accept and embrace you for who you are and not just how they want to see you. How can you stay true to yourself? First, get to know yourself and your interests, hobbies, values and beliefs. Ensure that nothing or no one influences your understanding of who you are. Second, share your beliefs with trusted individuals and observe their reactions. They don't have to agree with you, but they should accept you without criticism. Thirdly, take time to reflect on your beliefs and the people who respect them. Surround yourself with people who love and accept you for who you are, not who they want you to be. Develop a daily affirmation or mantra that you can recite before starting each day. This can serve as a powerful tool to motivate and boost your confidence.

To emphasise the idea that you are unwavering in keeping true to yourself, practise saying your affirmation aloud in front of a mirror. This mind-set will demonstrate strength of character that is becoming increasingly rare in today's society. When you are confident, criticism from others or society won't have much impact on you. Your true friends will encourage you to stay true to your beliefs and support you when you stand up against those who oppose you. Each of us has been uniquely created with the potential to make a significant impact on the world through our unique ideas. Don't give them up just because others may not understand or appreciate them. Take a stand, lead the way and show the world your authentic self.

4.6. EMBRACING AUTHENTICITY

Every now and then, we come across people with different or new traditions. It can be fun to try something different, as long as it's not destructive or violent. Traditions bring people together and foster strong connections within a group through shared celebrations. Each family in society has their own distinct traditions that set them apart from others, and that's okay. We should not judge a tradition that brings people together in harmony and peace and strengthens them. It's always enlightening to learn about the history and origins of a tradition. People within families and communities have their own perspectives and understandings concerning the world.

While some traditions evolve and change over time, others are held onto for a lifetime. Examples of widely celebrated traditions include Christmas and Easter, while others are specific to countries or religions, such as Ramadan, Hanukkah, Kwanza, Independence Day, Bonfire Night and Lent. It is also wise to consider that if we observe a particular dynamic that could be painful or forceful to people because they are not given freedom to express their identity, it is necessary to challenge the person responsible for enforcing such a dynamic. This will prevent them from oppressing others who wish to express their beliefs. Every day, we encounter numerous opinions and comments from society about how we should behave, what we should like and dislike and even how we should react to certain situations. While it's okay for others to express their opinions, it's important to remember that we, too, have the right to have different perspectives and opinions.

However, when expressing our views, it is crucial to communicate them respectfully and without resorting to yelling or aggression. Such behaviour not only frustrates the person speaking but also makes it difficult for the listener to understand, leading to unproductive conversations. Although standing up for one's beliefs may lead to disagreements and even insults, many people find that staying true to themselves leads to greater satisfaction than hiding behind a mask to impress others. At the end of the day, the choice is yours - whether you want to embrace your true self or deny who you were created to be. People have different beliefs and practices when it comes to religion and spirituality. While religious extremism and violence are never acceptable, those who find peace and love in their faith should not be discouraged.

If people's beliefs bring them fulfilment, it's important to accept and respect that, even if those beliefs don't align with your own. It's impossible to change someone else's beliefs, but we can choose to embrace our own.

Society's beliefs and trends don't have to dictate our own; it's about what makes sense to us based on all the information and perspectives we've considered. If our beliefs don't align with societal norms, it's okay to be true to ourselves. Surrounding ourselves with supportive friends and family who accept us for who we are can provide us with the reassurance we need to pursue our own paths. Diversity is what makes the world a rich and interesting place, and not everyone should have the same views. How we identify ourselves is also important. There are several aspects of life, such as skills, abilities, loving character traits and gifts that can shape our identity. While sexuality can be a part of this, society often places too much emphasis on it. Our sexuality doesn't define our whole character; there is much more to us than that aspect of ourselves. Traits that can help build a kinder and more compassionate world rather than always focusing on our own sexual pleasure.

When making friends, it's important to make choices that align with our values and preferences. However, it's equally important to avoid using force or aggression to achieve them. Relationships, in particular, require mutual consent and respect. If someone we want in our life doesn't reciprocate those feelings, it's best to move forward by respecting their decision. Finding like-minded individuals to connect with can be a challenge, but the best way to do so is by being true to yourself and openly expressing your passions. By living authentically, you will attract the right people who share your beliefs and interests. During my journey of healing from trauma, I found my supportive community by staying true to myself and never compromising on my values. It can be difficult to remain steadfast in your beliefs in a society that tries to influence you. However, by developing inner strength and resilience, you can overcome any obstacle and proudly showcase your unique personality and individuality to the world. A famous quote from an American sitcom goes like this:

Every time someone steps up and says
who they are, the world becomes a better,
more interesting place.
(Brooklyn Nine-Nine, S5 E10 "Game Night" 2017)

05. Amidst Oppression

5.1. INSULTS AND CRITICISM

Everyone deserves to be treated with dignity and respect. Unfortunately, we will encounter individuals who cannot control their ego or pride and resort to insults, criticism and hating others. However, it's important to remember that abuse is never acceptable, regardless of the reason. Whether we are trying to get even, dealing with personal pain or struggling with stress, using psychological or physical violence will never resolve the issue; instead, it only causes harm.

You must have heard the saying, "Sticks and stones may break my bones, but words will never hurt me". This is not entirely true. Words can hurt people, whether they are written on paper or verbally spoken, and there is science to back this claim. "The Hidden Messages in Water" is a book authored by Dr Masaru Emoto, a Japanese scientist who extensively researched the transformation of crystal structures in water. He conducted research on how the molecular structure of water is affected by various factors, such as the environment, words, thoughts and sounds. He talks about an experiment in which he used high-speed photography to analyse the crystal structure of water when exposed to different words. In 1999, a book titled

"The Messages of Water" was published, featuring images of crystal structures captured through the use of magnetic resonance analysis technology and high-speed photography. The experiment conducted by Dr Masaru Emoto involved exposing glasses of water to various stimuli, such as words, pictures and songs, and subsequently freezing them. The ice crystals were examined using microscopic photography. The water that was exposed to positive and comforting words showed crystal structures that resembled beautiful snowflakes. The water that was exposed to harmful or insulting words showed crystal structures resembling sludge.

My mother conducted this experiment at home in 2009 while I was still living with her. She used two identical jars using fresh rice grains and clear tap water. I recall the phrases "Death," "Satan," "Demon," "Hate," and "Evil" written on the labels of the first jar. The phrases "God," "Jesus," "Love," "Faith" and "Hope" were written on the second jar. These two jars were placed overnight in a fridge for the same duration. The observed results were fascinating. The water in the first jar had black particles and mould growing on it, and the rice looked inedible. On the other hand, the water in the second jar appeared to be clearer and purer than when it first came out of the tap. Isn't that interesting?

The human body is made up of 70% water, much like how the Earth's surface is 70% covered in water. It can be tempting to engage in gossip and throw insults, especially when trying to fit in with popular groups. However, it is important to keep in mind the science experiment where insults cause mould to grow. Just as mould can be harmful to the object it grows on, insults can have long-lasting negative effects on those they are directed towards. Therefore, it is crucial to resist the temptation to insult others and instead choose to treat them with kindness and respect. Insults are not healthy for either the recipient or the sender, and it is important to make a conscious effort to avoid them. Let us strive to create a positive and respectful environment where everyone feels valued and appreciated.

5.2. WHEN FAMILY AND FRIENDS CHANGE

The betrayal of a close friend or family member can be one of life's most devastating experiences. When those we trust the most suddenly start hurling insults and mistreating us, it can leave us feeling worthless, defeated, confused and abandoned. It can be difficult to know how to respond when someone close to us treats us this way. Do we continue to put up with the abuse, or do we reduce interaction with them so that we can take care of ourselves?

When someone we have a close emotional bond with insults us, it can be more difficult to ignore or forget their hurtful words compared to a stranger's insults. Sometimes, it only takes one small disagreement or misunderstanding to change the dynamic of a relationship. Insults have no place in any form of friendship or relationship. Relationships should provide comfort instead of being a source of pain or harm. When faced with abuse, it is important to set boundaries to protect yourself. No one deserves to be subjected to abuse. This can involve reducing communication or distancing yourself from the person who is causing harm. By setting boundaries, we show those who have insulted or mistreated us that such behaviour is not acceptable. This will also give them time to reflect on their actions and make necessary changes. In an abusive relationship, hoping for a miracle is ineffective and rarely leads to improvement. You have the power to take control of the situation. Although it may be scary to take a stand against those who have hurt us, it is important to remember that by doing so, we can change the situation for the better. It may not be possible to change the situation immediately, but never dismiss the importance of speaking up, particularly when you are facing abuse from family or friends.

Here are a few key points to keep in mind: Your emotions and feelings are valid; you don't have to tolerate abuse, and you have the right to speak up for yourself. It's possible that the person who is treating you poorly is going through a difficult time and is unable to express their emotions in a healthy way. However, that doesn't excuse their behaviour, and it's important to set boundaries to protect yourself from their mistreatment.

No matter what someone is going through, it does not justify their mistreatment of you. Pain should always be expressed in a healthy and non-violent manner. Both men and women have the right to feel pain and express it in a safe manner. It's possible that after some time has passed, the people who abused you may come to their senses and treat you with respect again. At the end of the day, it's up to you to decide whether you want to continue to tolerate the mistreatment or stand up for yourself. The choice is yours, so think carefully about what's best for you.

5.3. DEALING WITH INSULTS AND EMOTIONAL TRAUMA FROM VERBAL OPPRESSION

It's common to face situations where others don't agree with our beliefs and values. This can be especially challenging when it comes from individuals who don't know us well or have only had limited interactions with us. Insults can be particularly hurtful when they are directed at us in the presence of others. However, it's important to be confident and secure in your own identity and not let their words define you. To achieve this, take the time to understand and embrace who you are so that the opinions of others have no power over you.

It's essential to make time for self-care so that you feel truly grounded and at ease with yourself. It may be tempting to prioritise work and responsibilities, but it's important to remember that taking care of yourself is crucial to effectively handle your responsibilities. Set boundaries and know your limits; don't let anyone pressure you into neglecting your own needs. Use your time off from work to recharge and rejuvenate. The stress and negativity from oppression can drain your energy and cause you to enter into a state of fight, flight or freeze mode, which can cloud your thinking and disconnect you from your authentic self. When stress and insults weigh heavily on you, it can be easy to slip into a defensive state of mind. However, it's still possible to be your true self, even in the face of opposition.

When it comes to finding your source of comfort, it's important to identify what resonates with you the most. Whether its music, exercise or a solo walk in nature, find what brings you to a place of safety. Having friends who listen and support you can also be incredibly helpful in easing the emotional weight you might be carrying. Although your friends will help you, it's crucial that you also play a role in stabilising yourself. If there's something that you know fuels your positivity, hold onto it and let it rejuvenate you. I listen to a few songs that motivate me to stay strong when people oppress me. You might have your own set of personal songs that help you stay strong. The following are some of my favourites related to standing strong in the midst of oppression:

- "Brave" by Sara Bareilles (2013)
- "Stronger (What Doesn't Kill You)" by Kelly Clarkson (2012)
- "Fight Song" by Rachel Patten (2014)
- "So Am I" by Ava Max (2019)

Oppression, particularly from those we are close to, can be frightening, especially when they attempt to enlist others in their cause. It can be easy to feel overwhelmed in such situations, but it's important to remember that the size of a group does not determine the accuracy of their beliefs. Confidence in your beliefs and recognising that insults are mere attempts to tear you down will make it easier to not let them affect you.

5.4. NOWHERE TO RUN OR HIDE?

The biggest challenge when facing oppression is finding a safe haven. A prime example of this is when a young child experiences abuse from their parents and feels like there's no place to escape to so that they can decompress. Unfortunately, in many cases, the abuse and oppression continue because the victim can't find a safe space. Some people, however, have been lucky enough to find solace, be it at a friend's house, a family member's house or when the abuse was brought to the right authorities and dealt with appropriately. No one wants to be around someone who makes them feel small, but it's saddening when people don't take the necessary steps to mitigate the harm. For some people, fear has been instilled so deeply that they believe that enduring the abuse is their only option. It's important to remember that every traumatic experience we go through is recorded by our bodies and minds and can trigger a reaction or behaviour when something in life reminds us of that situation. Sometimes, even small triggers can lead to a panic attack. For example, a slight touch on the hand can be overwhelming for someone who has experienced physical abuse. A harmless joke can be distressing for someone who has been laughed at and humiliated in the past. Entering a situation that resembles a traumatic event can also be triggering. Similarly, taking away a possession without consent can be upsetting for someone who has had valuable items stolen or taken from them. While solutions can be found, it's important to weigh the consequences before taking action.

When children face abuse from their parents, there are two options available: separating the child from the parent or keeping them together. While separating the child from their parent can provide them with a safe and abuse-free environment, it can also result in the trauma of separation from family, which might cause behavioural difficulties. On the other hand, if the child remains with the abusive parent, they will continue to experience harm and trauma. Both options have their consequences, and each will take an emotional toll on the child. The person making this choice must think about all the outcomes and make the best decision for everyone involved. When you are oppressed as an adult and feel like you have nowhere else to turn, it's important to have at least one person you can turn to for support. Having someone who truly cares for you and wants to help, such as a close friend or family member, can make a world of difference in overcoming oppressive situations. Look for those individuals who offer encouragement, like "I'm with you till the end" or "You can always come to me" and make efforts to build strong, supportive relationships with them. Having a trustworthy person to turn to during challenging times can provide the strength and comfort you need to keep going and overcome difficulties.

5.5. AN UNSETTLING TRUTH

Sometimes, it's necessary to confront truths that dispel the illusions and misconceptions we hold. These truths can be difficult to hear, but they serve to bring us back to reality. By seeing the world for what it truly is, we can better understand and address its challenges, including the ugliness and injustices that exist. When it comes to family, friends and the oppression we may face from them, it's important to acknowledge that not everyone will agree with us. There will be people in our lives who won't understand our perspectives and may not even try to understand them, and this can be particularly difficult if those people are close to us. By facing reality, we can build our inner strength and resilience so that we are better equipped to handle challenges and oppression. Unfortunately, even worse, some people won't care about our feelings even when we're hurting, despite the fact that we all wish for a more compassionate world. To those who have experienced this kind of heartache, I offer my sincere condolences. It takes strength and resilience to keep standing strong in the face of such challenges.

The sudden change in behaviour from those who were once close to us can feel like a profound betrayal. The thought of your closest circle suddenly turning against you can be unsettling. However, if you have been honest, truthful and treated those people with love and respect, then their actions are a reflection of their issues and not a reflection of any wrongdoing on your part. It can be easy to feel like you've done something wrong when your oppressors use lies and manipulation to control you. The best thing you can do in such situations is to calmly ask them what it is that you've done wrong. If the response is illogical or inconsistent with your past behaviour, then it's important to not internalise their insults and to stand firm in your own truth. As I recently experienced myself, it's a common occurrence to unintentionally trigger someone's emotions. Even when we believe we are communicating effectively and have good intentions, the other person may still misunderstand us and leave us feeling confused. It's natural to feel unsure or to wonder, "Where did I go wrong?" or "Is this all my fault?". However, it's important to remember that how people respond to challenging situations, whether peacefully or aggressively, is a reflection of their own choices and not a reflection of our actions. The person who reacts must take full responsibility for their response. In these cases, acknowledging their actions and taking steps to make amends can help repair the relationship.

The emphasis placed on appearance in today's world is undeniable. From sleek cars to attractive homes and good-looking individuals, we're often drawn to what is visually appealing. However, it's important to remember that looks can be deceiving. It's tempting to be drawn to what is aesthetically pleasing, but it's not always a reliable indicator of what's truly on the inside. Have you ever been in a situation where something or someone appeared to be perfect, only for you to discover hidden flaws that caused disappointment and even depression? How often have you fallen into this trap? It is not uncommon to encounter people who initially seem innocent, only to later reveal a dark side of their personality, causing chaos. These individuals often referred to as "wolves in sheep's clothing," can be difficult to identify. While a beautiful exterior can be enticing, it's equally important to examine the person's heart and character. A kind and loving personality can make someone shine even brighter. As a Christian, I have learned from the Bible that God values inner qualities, such as the heart, over outward appearance (The Bible - 1 Samuel 16:7).

5.6. HOW WE STAND STRONG

So, what can we do during times of oppression that make us feel like the whole world is against us? It can seem like no one wants to listen to our side of the story, and that there's nobody to love us. During such times, it's important to remember that no one is meant to go through life alone. Although some people may have a tendency towards introversion and prefer to be alone, deep down, humans are social creatures and need social interaction and connection to thrive. Believing that we can handle everything on our own can lead to feelings of extreme loneliness. During difficult times, it is crucial to connect with individuals who genuinely care about us and are willing to listen and provide support. Whether it's through friends, family or community support groups, finding someone who can provide a sense of comfort and understanding can help us navigate through these challenging times. Also take the time to get to know yourself. Understanding your flaws, strengths, weaknesses and skills will give you the confidence to say, "I know myself better than anyone else." When you have a solid understanding of yourself, false statements made by others will seem invalid and unimportant. This will reduce the impact of negative comments, as you'll know that they are based on false assumptions. When you are self-aware, you will project a strong and confident image of yourself that is not influenced by the opinions of others. Taking time for introspection is crucial for personal growth and happiness. We need to understand our strengths, weaknesses and skills to become the best versions of ourselves. No one is perfect, but continuously working on self-improvement can bring about a positive change. It's important to ignore external opinions and focus on what brings fulfilment in our lives. This self-awareness will also help in not being affected by negative or false statements from those who may seek to oppress us. By getting to know ourselves, we build inner strength and resilience.

Another important consideration during times of oppression is the choice between living in fear and living in love. As previously mentioned, love drives out fear, as they cannot coexist. If you are being criticised, belittled and made to feel upset by someone, where do you think they are coming from - a place of love or fear? In my experience, some of my friends have come to me in tears, feeling hurt by insults directed towards them despite their best efforts to handle a difficult situation with their oppressors. My friends, who were talented, kind, considerate and had so much to offer, were sometimes met with insults and criticism instead of praise and recognition for their abilities. It can be difficult to understand why someone would want to bring down someone who has so much to offer. However, sometimes people feel threatened by those who are talented and successful. Some individuals, even if they don't feel directly threatened, may still feel threatened by the perceived competition and strive to "eliminate" it. This is a reflection of their own insecurities and is not a reflection of the character or worth of the person being attacked. If you're aware that your oppressors want to bring you down because they're scared of your abilities, you don't have to respond with retaliation. Instead, you can be strong in yourself and understand that it is fear that is driving your oppressors. Remain true to yourself and continue to work on becoming the best version of yourself.

06. Facing Rejection

6.1. HUMAN NATURE

Let's talk about the way, we humans, naturally react and behave in different situations. Some of these behaviours can be thought of as a default program in our minds that can be altered over time, while others are inherent traits that we carry with us throughout our lives and cannot be changed.

It's common for humans to have a wide range of emotions. We often show strong emotions, like happiness, excitement, anger or rage. Our thoughts and feelings can be overwhelming at times, and we need to manage them carefully. Emotions come in many forms, from romantic attraction when we see someone attractive to anger when we're insulted, from excitement when we receive gifts to sadness when we lose someone we love. These emotions are a natural part of the human experience. We often act impulsively based on our emotions without considering the consequences. This can lead to hasty decisions and actions that may not align with our logic. While expressing emotions is a vital aspect of human behaviour, societal norms and expectations can sometimes dictate how men and women should express themselves emotionally. Men are often told to "man up" or "be a man" when they experience negative emotions, which can be damaging to their mental and emotional well-being. In contrast, women are rarely told to "woman up." Many people believe that men are not supposed to cry or be vulnerable and that they are supposed to suppress their emotions. This societal pressure to suppress emotions can lead to pent-up feelings and sudden outbursts, which can harm our mental health and lead to suicide.

Suicide is a heartbreaking and devastating outcome of intense emotional distress. It is a clear indication that an individual no longer wants to experience life due to overwhelming feelings of anger or sadness. Unfortunately, this tragedy occurs all too frequently. In 2021, the Centers for Disease Control and Prevention (CDC) reported 48,183 suicides in the US, with 36,551 of them being male. Additionally, 12.3 million adults reported having suicidal thoughts. These statistics emphasise the need for individuals to feel comfortable expressing their emotions and seek support when needed. On the subject of rejection, let's focus on how people react to it. We may face rejection in many different situations: when we apply for a job, when we ask someone on a date, when we ask for something from someone, when we offer our services, etc. To be honest, rejection is tough to handle. As mentioned earlier in the book, the water experiment showed that negative words can affect the formation of water crystals, and similarly, rejection can make us feel negative emotions such as anger, sadness, frustration and disappointment.

It's normal to feel upset or angry when facing rejection, and having a supportive network can help to provide comfort and help regulate our emotions. If you have experienced severe rejection, I want you to know that it's okay to give yourself grace and comfort. It's easy to fall into the trap of negative self-talk when you experience rejection, but it's important to remember that these thoughts are often not rooted in truth. In the past, I've struggled with managing my emotions after being rejected, but a video from author Teal Swan helped me understand that rejection doesn't define my worth, expressing emotions doesn't make me weak and that rejection can be an opportunity for personal growth. If you'd like to learn more about overcoming rejection, I highly recommend watching "How to Handle Rejection - Teal Swan" on YouTube. Now that we know how rejection makes us feel, we must learn how to manage our extreme reactions to rejection in a healthy way.

6.2. THE TRUE MEASURE OF STRENGTH

People believe that strength is derived from the number of victories they achieve. However, I believe that this is a perception shaped by our ego. When we put our ego aside and reflect on situations objectively, we realise that winning is not always the defining factor of strength. The true test of strength lies in the ability to rise from defeat and overcome hardships. In my experience, it is these challenges that lead me to the greatest growth and personal development. Defeat and rejection are two experiences that nobody wants, for they cause similar feelings of disappointment and frustration. While no one likes to lose or experience rejection, they are an inevitable part of life. Sharing our hardships with others is a testament to our growth, especially if we can stand tall in terms of a roof over our head, being surrounded by loved ones and having good health. It's natural to feel angry or frustrated after experiencing a loss or rejection, but it's important to keep our emotions in check. Acting out in aggression, whether through shouting, throwing objects, violence or destroying property, only causes further harm and has no positive outcome.

When we feel tempted to express our anger in an aggressive manner, it's important to find healthier ways to channel our emotions. Anger is a natural emotion, but it's when we resist the urge to act on it that we truly demonstrate our strength. It can be tempting to seek revenge on the ones who hurt us as a way to release our anger. When we experience pain, it's a natural reaction to want someone else to feel the same pain we do. We've all heard expressions like "getting a taste of their own medicine" or "karma." But acting on this urge will never bring true satisfaction or happiness. By finding healthy ways to express our anger, we can gain greater emotional strength and handle rejection and loss more effectively. When anger takes over, it can lead to irrational behaviour and a loss of control, creating a cycle where anger dominates us instead of the other way around. It's easy to get caught up in the moment and, as they say, "lose our heads". Films like Raimi's "Spider-Man 3," depict how wanting to seek revenge can bring out the worst in us and make us unpleasant individuals. This film has an interesting quote:

Revenge; it's like a poison. It can take you over.
Before you know it, turns us into something ugly.
(Spider-Man 3, 2007)

I've come across people with varying views on managing anger. Some think its okay to lash out destructively, while others believe anger should be kept in check.

However, what's important is finding a healthy balance, where it's possible to express anger without causing harm to oneself or others. To achieve this, there are various activities you can do to release stress in a healthy way. The science behind feelings of rejection or anger is rooted in our body's natural response to stress - the sympathetic mode (fight, flight or freeze) as previously mentioned in the book. When we experience strong emotions like anger or rejection, our body's stress response is triggered, leading to an increase in the heart rate, blood pressure and body temperature. This is the "fight-or-flight" response that would help us survive dangerous situations.

However, in situations where there is no immediate physical danger, it's important to learn how to manage these emotions effectively. There are various methods to help regulate our emotions and they are definitely worth learning.

6.3. YOUR RELATIONSHIPS

The most hurtful type of rejection occurs when it's from those closest to us, such as family and friends. It may even come from someone we have romantic feelings for. These relationships hold great emotional importance, and rejection can cause deep emotional pain. In a sense, our hearts are intricately tied to those we love, and when they cause us harm, it feels like a physical blow to the heart. Rejection is an inevitable part of life, and it's a difficult experience to go through, especially when it comes from those we consider to be our closest loved ones. When someone tries their best to be kind and still gets rejected, it can leave a deep emotional wound that can be difficult to heal from. This is a situation that I, like many others, have faced with family and friends.

Have you ever experienced feelings of exclusion or neglect? Perhaps you were left out of a social event, like a party or special occasion or didn't receive an invitation to a gathering or party from someone you considered a close friend. This can lead to feelings of insecurity and questions about your place in the friendship, and whether you did anything to upset them. It's common for people's opinions and feelings about you to change over time. This can be especially painful when it involves someone we thought we were close to. For example, being excluded from significant events like birthdays, anniversaries or weddings after having spent a lot of time building a connection and having meaningful conversations with a friend can be painful and leave you feeling ignored or unvalued. However, my perspective changed after a chance encounter on a bus ride to work in Coventry. I met a woman, and we chatted on four separate bus rides, during which we had enjoyable, albeit random, conversations. To my surprise, she later invited me to her wedding and reception, despite having only met four times. This experience was eye-opening for me, as it highlighted the difference between people who value me in their lives and those who don't.

There are times when we may feel rejected and unloved, especially when a friend or family member doesn't acknowledge us as much as we would like. I have friends who go for months or even years without talking to me, but when we do finally reconnect, it feels as if no time has passed. These friendships often last a lifetime, and I truly value them. However, I have also experienced situations where I was the one putting in all the effort to maintain a friendship, and I noticed that even though my friends claimed to be busy, their social media activity showed otherwise. This led me to question where I stood in their lives. I have learned that I should never settle for a friend who doesn't willingly make an effort to interact with me. We need people who make us feel loved and express genuine interest in us. As mentioned in the book, "The Hidden Messages in Water", a fascinating discovery about water crystals is that they turn into sludge-like structures not only when subjected to insults but also when ignored. This is similar to how our bodies feel when we experience rejection, as our bodies are mostly composed of water. With our bodies being comprised of 70% water, it's easy to understand how being insulted or ignored can negatively impact our physical and emotional health.

While reflecting on your relationships, consider this question: Have you ever felt rejected or ignored by a specific family member or friend? Have you ever held back emotions that you wanted to express to them? Do you feel invisible in their presence? It's okay to speak up and express how you feel. Communication is key in any relationship and the right friends and family will listen and provide the love and recognition you deserve. Don't be afraid to speak up and address any issues that may be causing a strain in your relationship.

6.4. COMMON LIFE SCENARIOS

Let's examine some everyday scenarios where rejection may occur so that we can become more aware of its manifestation and how to react. As previously discussed, rejection can present itself in various forms, especially in our relationships with friends and family. This can take the form of a sudden decrease in communication, being excluded from events or milestones or feeling disregarded. In the realm of romantic and sexual relationships, rejection can be a prevalent theme. People are often preoccupied with their romantic and sexual partners, and the attention given to this type of relationship often overshadows other relationships. In casual conversations, people often share their thoughts and experiences on this topic, including both positive and negative experiences. Rejection is a common experience in the realm of love and relationships, regardless of whether the individuals involved are in a committed relationship or not.

People's experiences of rejection can vary widely, with some feeling discouraged and unhappy while others being able to quickly move on. It's common to hear discussions about rejection and speculation on why one person was rejected while another was not. Some individuals experience a strong physical and emotional attraction towards someone they've just met, and despite getting to know them better over time, they still hold a desire to pursue a romantic relationship with them. Rejection can be more challenging to handle when there is a strong emotional bond involved. Unfortunately, it can also result in negative self-talk, such as self-doubt, self-hatred and self-sabotage. To prevent these negative outcomes, it's crucial to identify the warning signs and address them before they escalate.

Even after marriage and having children, disagreements, disputes, and lack of consideration can cause a relationship to break down. Divorce is common in today's society and can leave those involved feeling distraught and psychologically wounded. In response to the pain caused by break-ups and rejection, some may choose to close themselves off, but this is not a healthy solution. By shutting off vulnerability, one may miss out on the opportunity to form the best relationships possible and limit the potential for future relationships. Furthermore, closing oneself off can lead to sabotaging current relationships and throwing aside parts of one's own identity, which can impact many areas of life.

Applying for jobs can be a trying process. Sending out countless applications, participating in multiple interviews and the constant effort to put ourselves out there can take a toll on our mental well-being. It's not uncommon to face rejections, especially if you're trying to advance your career and pursue your passion. I've experienced many rejections and have sent countless applications in an attempt to break into my desired industry. The rejection can lead to self-doubt and negative thoughts, such as "I'm not good enough". "I've missed my chance", or "Someone else will beat me." These thoughts can make us believe we are unworthy of the positions we aspire to. This can be especially disheartening when we're striving to earn a livelihood. However, it's important to remember that there is someone out there who will appreciate our skills, personality and portfolio. There's a job out there for everyone who is willing to put in the effort. It took me years to land the job I was looking for, when I was passionate, enthusiastic and determined in my job search, I eventually landed the job I was looking for. If I can do it, you definitely can. Don't give up, and trust in yourself that you have what it takes to succeed.

6.5. RELEASING THE EMOTIONS (SAFE HOUSE)

A book that helped me realise the importance of expressing our emotions in a healthy way is "The Chimp Paradox" by Prof Steve Peters. When we experience stress, our bodies go into the sympathetic mode, releasing hormones that create a rush of energy. Instead of lashing out, channel this energy into physical activities that can bring you peace. This could be anything from hitting a punching bag to running or even dancing. Dancing can be a great stress-reliever because it allows us to express ourselves freely and shake off the stress through physical movement. In the words of a famous song, "Shake it off!" (Taylor Swift, 2014).

Some individuals prefer to adopt a more tranquil approach when dealing with stress. As long as their chosen method doesn't cause harm to themselves or others, they should continue to do so. For example, taking a peaceful walk in nature can be calming. Engaging in therapeutic activities like painting, singing or any other creative art can also help process negative emotions and alleviate grief. Talking to others can also be effective in releasing and processing emotions. You may choose to spend time with trusted friends, family or anyone who accepts your authentic self. Sometimes, all you need is for someone to acknowledge your emotions and offer love and support. However, if you are experiencing deep stress, going to therapy or counselling sessions can help you understand and work through your emotions. These sessions can also help you identify the root cause of your emotions. Though it can be difficult to address these issues, the sense of freedom that you will feel after processing them is unparalleled and can greatly improve your mental and emotional well-being. When facing stress, some people turn to unhealthy coping mechanisms such as drugs, alcohol, self-harm, porn and uncontrollable anger. While such behaviour may provide temporary relief, they can easily spiral into destructive habits that cause harm to our physical and mental well-being. For example, excessive alcohol consumption can harm our liver and physical health, while excessive use of porn can impact our perceptions and relationships, causing feelings of shame and loneliness. Self-harm can cause physical scars and increase feelings of isolation and despair, whereas relying too much on the internet and magazines can cause emotional instability and a sense of dependence. It's important to recognise the dangers of these coping mechanisms and seek healthier ways to deal with stress.

It's important to stay aware of the effects of stress-relieving activities on your well-being. While these activities can help manage stress, it's possible to become overly dependent on them. If you sense that a stress-relieving activity is starting to take over your life or have negative consequences, it's important to take action. Reach out to trusted friends, family or a mental health professional for support. They can help you evaluate the situation and find healthier alternatives. Their input can be valuable in determining if an activity is benefiting you or not. Remember, the goal is to maintain balance and control and not to lose yourself in the process of managing stress.

6.6. ACCEPTANCE

Rejection can be a difficult experience, but it is possible to move past it. The five stages of grief offer a structure to help deal with the emotions that come after rejection. Although each stage can be difficult, working through them can lead to healing and release from emotional pain. It takes effort and commitment to process the hurt.

To remind you of the five stages of grief: Stage one is denial, where we dismiss the truth and refuse to believe the reality that is happening to us. Stage two is anger, where we may feel intense rage and often direct it towards someone or something. Stage three is bargaining, where we may attempt to make a deal or exchange in the hopes that our giving will make us feel better, or we may dwell on wondering if there's something we could have done better in the situation that has happened to us. Stage four is depression, where we may experience deep sadness and feel as though there is no hope left for us as we come to terms with the painful truth that has hurt us. Stage five is acceptance, where, over time, we process the pain and sadness and no longer try to fight or change the situation. We know that what has happened has happened, and we have the strength to move forward in our lives.

Any event that can be emotionally or psychologically traumatic for us can leave a lasting impact and trigger feelings of discomfort in the future. While it may be difficult to confront the root causes of our negative emotions, doing so can also lead to healing and growth.

During the COVID-19 pandemic, I realised that I had gone through more trauma than I previously acknowledged. At first, I was in denial and resisted facing the truths about myself and my experiences. However, when I finally accepted the dark truths about myself and the abuses that I was subjected to, I felt a profound sense of release and freedom. My confidence grew. I trusted my intuition more. I became more comfortable in my skin, and I took more risks. I also became more focused, worked harder and became wiser about setting boundaries. I became aware of how to show kindness and love to others while protecting myself from further harm. So, if you're ready, take the time to examine the root causes of your emotions. The rewards can be truly transformative. The loss of close relationships can leave deep emotional scars, especially when they end in betrayal or insult. I had to come to terms with several difficult realities about lost friendships and relationships over time to be better equipped for future heartache. Here are some reflections that may be helpful to you:

- Life is a journey of growth and change, and our paths may sometimes diverge from others as a result. This is a natural occurrence
- Some individuals may only be meant to be a part of our lives for a specific period of time, serving a purpose and then moving on
- The right people will stay in our lives and make their presence felt through their love and support
- As others leave, new people enter our lives and bring new opportunities for growth and connection
- It's okay to let go of people who are no longer bringing positivity to your life. There will always be others who will bring joy and fulfilment
- People have their own lives to lead, and it's important to not let the fact that they have moved on impact you in a negative way. Take time to process your emotions, and be open to new possibilities

The pain of abandonment by friends who we thought would always be there for us is devastating. They may have once expressed their love and support for us, but then suddenly act as if they don't even know us or have become our enemies. I've also had friends who grew apart from me, and while their insults once hurt, I learned to brush them off. They only knew an outdated version of me, and I've come to understand that we all change and grow, often in remarkable ways, when we invest in ourselves. We become more confident in who we are and what's true or false about us. If strangers or those who haven't invested in our growth try to bring us down, we don't need to take their insults to heart, especially if they don't know our story.

The pain of rejection is intense and can even affect our physical health. "Broken Heart Syndrome" is a real condition that occurs when severe emotional trauma affects the heart, causing it to malfunction and even stop working. However, by taking care of our emotions, healing our past trauma and giving ourselves love, we can minimise the risk of experiencing a literal broken heart. Here's a quote from a Marvel film that I always think about whenever I reflect on my life and the choices I make:

Whatever comes our way, whatever battle we have raging inside us, we always have a choice... It's the choices that make us who we are, and we can always choose to do what's right.

(Spider-Man 3, 2007)

07. Whilst Venturing

7.1. ADVENTURES IN THE WORLD

The contrast between the two well-known phrases "small world" and "it's a big world out there," highlights the differing perspectives we hold on while exploring the world. There are so many places that are waiting to be discovered and explored, such as the ones we read about, the ones that were recommended to us, the ones we see on TV or the ones that are discovered by chance. Some individuals are avid travellers, seeking adventure both within their own country and beyond, but their willingness to step outside of their comfort zone ultimately dictates how far they venture. While the vastness of the world can seem intimidating and negative headlines cast a shadow over certain countries, it is important to remember that every destination has its unique challenges and difficulties. Limiting our travel horizons can result in missed opportunities and experiences that have the potential to enrich our lives.

Travel was never a priority for me until my final year of university. Despite advising to concentrate on my education and future career, my parents introduced me to the joys of travel through vacations abroad. It wasn't until I took a part in a three-month volunteering opportunity at a summer camp in Maine, USA, that I fully realised my passion for travel. After my volunteering work was over,

I had the chance to explore New York and Chicago on my own. The experience was freeing, as I encountered wonderful people, tasted exquisite food and marvelled at breathtaking sights. I made memories that will stay with me forever. My brief glimpse into the American culture as a Briton only intensified my desire to explore more of the world and seek out new and thrilling travel experiences.

While I was away, I had moments of introspection where I took the time to reflect on my life and my goals. This gave me an opportunity to think about what I truly wanted in life, what I valued, who I wanted in my support system and how I could bring more fulfilment and purpose into my life. Often, our daily routines and responsibilities can consume us, leaving us feeling like we're on autopilot. However, it's important to periodically check in with ourselves to ensure that we're truly happy with our choices and not just going through the motions of what's expected of us. Neglecting these inner desires can result in negative emotions cropping up in unexpected ways. Although solo trips can be incredible experiences, it's not always possible to uncover all the hidden gems on our own. The people we meet and interact with can often offer insights and directions that we might have overlooked otherwise. Many times, I felt discouraged when I saw my friends posting about their vacations with their friends on social media. It was difficult for me to find someone who wanted to accompany me on these trips, whether it was in my local area or abroad.

However, I refused to let the lack of company stop me from getting those experiences that helped me understand who I am. I have no regrets about all the trips I've taken so far, even if there were some challenges. For those who may not be comfortable travelling alone, I encourage you to find a way to explore the world. You'll gain a deeper appreciation for what's out there. Just like me, you may meet people who will help you rediscover yourself and bring new perspectives and love into your life. Life is meant for us to grow and discover, not to be stuck in a routine with unchecked emotions. As the saying goes, "Life is an adventure". Keep exploring and you might be surprised at what you find.

7.2. ADVENTURES IN YOUR MIND

Taking a journey into your own mind can be a valuable exercise in self-reflection and understanding. During this process, you can examine your thoughts, beliefs and emotions. This self-reflection can help you determine your priorities and aspirations in life, as well as areas where you are succeeding and areas where you need to work on. It's important to remember that perfection is not attainable and its okay to acknowledge that there are aspects of your life that need improvement.

Throughout my life, I discovered several hobbies and pastimes that allowed me to connect with my true interests and self. It all started with watching TV shows and films, which not only entertained me but also helped me understand my taste in media. Over time, I developed a passion for creative and artistic hobbies, such as painting and drawing, as I loved the idea of bringing something to life from a blank canvas. These hobbies gave me a sense of control and creativity, which in turn re-energised me to face the world. I discovered model building through Airfix brand model kits. This hobby piqued my interest in the 3D world and allowed me to gain an appreciation for the magnificent structures that fly overhead. It also sparked my career aspirations in the aircraft industry. That was when I discovered I wanted to work closely with aircraft in my future career. My model-building skills advanced through university, where I developed the ability to build models from scratch without relying on instruction manuals. This was a big step for me as an engineer. In recent years, I have found a new hobby in cosplay and regularly attend comic conventions to show off my creations, such as costumes and film props, and meet like-minded friends.

My hobbies have played a significant role in shaping my passions and direction in both my personal and professional life. Through painting, drawing, crafting and walking in the mountains, I've been able to reflect on important life questions and explore my true desires. These activities have provided me with a peaceful space to think, free from outside influence and expectations. Walking in nature, in particular, has given me a unique perspective on the world and opened my mind to new possibilities. I've been able to reflect on past experiences, both good and bad and consider the kind of friends, lifestyle and future I want to build. In addition to these hobbies, music has also played a huge part in my journey of self-discovery. It has allowed me to explore my taste in music and discover songs that speak to me on a deeper level. These songs often evoke thoughts and emotions that lead me to reflect on myself and my life direction. However, I recognise that many people often sacrifice their individuality to fit into society's expectations or to please others. I believe it's important to find the right friendship circle, but this shouldn't come at the cost of sacrificing the best parts of who you are. Having a unique mind-set might set us apart from the crowd, but it's important to consider if we will truly be happy if we try to become like everyone else.

7.3. TAKING TIME OUT

It's essential to take breaks and prioritise self-care. We are not computers that can run endlessly without rest; we need sleep to recharge and replenish our energy. Regular self-care time not only helps us recharge but also allows us to work to the best of our abilities. Ignoring the need for self-care can have serious consequences. At some point in our lives, whether due to illness or injury, our bodies may tell us to slow down. If we continue to push ourselves beyond our limits, we risk our bodies failing altogether. It's essential to listen to our bodies and take the necessary time to recover and heal. If you're feeling pain or discomfort that prevents you from completing tasks, it's a clear sign that it's time to slow down. Your body needs time to repair itself, and ignoring the signs can lead to further damage. It's important to take some time off to regain your strength and be able to work effectively. This is also a message that many medical professionals would likely support.

We all experience moments in life when we need to hit the pause button and prioritise self-care. Whether it's due to physical injury, medical illness or simply having a schedule that's packed to the brim, taking time for ourselves is crucial for maintaining a healthy balance. When we get caught up in a repetitive routine, it can feel like we're stuck in a never-ending cycle, just like the film "Groundhog Day" portrays. It's all too common to have a schedule that prioritises caring for our children, working non-stop or looking after others, leaving little room for our own needs and those of our loved ones. However, ignoring our own well-being can have negative consequences, leading to a life that's out of balance. That's why I encourage you to take a close look at your schedule and acknowledge if you have taken on too much. If you need to process a feeling, sort out your priorities or attend to a pressing matter, don't hesitate to realign your priorities. After all, your life belongs to you, and you have the power to decide how to shape it.

Reminding yourself to take time for self-care and recharge is an important step, but it's not enough unless you take action. Just like others need breaks, you do too. If you realise that you need some time for yourself or to attend to an area of your life that needs your attention, speak up, and let your support circle know. They should love and support you enough to understand that you need a break. When you secure your regular self-care time, use it wisely. Whether it's time with your partner, kids or engaging in a personal activity that helps you stay connected to yourself, having a plan can clarify what you need to do. Make sure your time slot is reasonable and that no one is rushing you. You deserve to take your time, especially after giving your all to others. Remember that you're not a machine that can run 24/7. All humans need sleep and rest to process, and you can't perform at your best without it. So, give yourself the same grace and devotion that you give to others.

7.4. SHARING YOUR JOURNEY

Throughout my life journey and travels to various places, I've had the privilege of meeting a diverse group of people who have shared their unique stories with me. These experiences have broadened my understanding of the different lives and cultures that exist in the world. I found great joy in getting to know people from all over the world. While the people I met shared both heart-warming and difficult stories about their lives, I understand that sharing painful experiences can be challenging and trigger trauma experienced in the past.

It's understandable if you don't feel comfortable talking about those experiences, but it's important to recognise that bottling such heavy emotions can have a negative impact on your well-being. Healing from trauma can lead to feeling lighter and unburdened, allowing you to live a healthier, happier life. You don't have to rush the process and it can happen at its own pace, but it's important to acknowledge that it needs to happen. Facing your past can be intimidating, but it also has the potential to reveal the inner strength and resilience that you possess. It can be a journey of self-discovery and personal growth. Sharing your story with others can inspire others to tap into their inner strengths and create a safe space for others to open up about their struggles and trauma. Your journey can be a source of inspiration and healing for yourself and others.

Carrying the weight of trauma can have negative effects on our mental and emotional well-being. It is common for people to keep their traumatic experiences to themselves, especially in a world where respect and understanding can be lacking. Sharing our traumatic experiences can be challenging, as it reveals a vulnerable side of ourselves that we fear may be used against us. However, opening up about our experiences can be a step towards healing. By sharing initial or surface-level details of our experiences, we can gauge the level of openness and empathy of the person we are speaking with. Gradually, we may feel comfortable enough to share more intimate details. In any relationship, vulnerability is crucial. Sharing the truth about ourselves, even if it exposes our weaknesses, is the only way to allow love in. Life is a journey full of adventures and growth. Along the way, we explore the world and search for moments of happiness to add to our lives. At times, we need to be alone to process and heal our wounds, but it's also important to share these experiences with our loved ones. Our relationships with friends and family can enrich our personal growth and self-discovery, as we are inherently social beings who thrive on human connection. They bring depth to our stories and experiences, and their support can help us navigate the challenges of life. After all, no one can truly make it through life completely alone. Even those who claim to enjoy being alone have at least a few close relationships.

At celebrations, holidays and other milestones, we want to be surrounded by those closest to us. Sharing these moments with loved ones makes them even more special and creates memories that can be treasured forever. This is why many people seek a life partner to share their experiences with. During difficult times, it's important to have a strong support system of friends and family who can provide comfort and understanding, as well as wise advice for growth. Sharing our stories and experiences with these supportive people can lead to growth and self-discovery in unexpected ways. This has been my experience, and I have found strength that I never thought was possible. While I am still a work-in-progress, I am confident that my healing journey has improved many aspects of my life. I am grateful for everyone who has been a part of my journey and helped me get to where I am today. The challenges from my foes and support from my friends have allowed me to discover my strength. If I can be transformed for the better, so can you. Surrounding yourself with loved ones will lead to a more fulfilling and meaningful life.

7.5. WORK HARD/PLAY HARD

In life, it's essential to strike a balance between our responsibilities and having fun. To prevent burnout, breakdowns and emotional outbursts, it's crucial to give ourselves the right amount of leisure time along with our work. The average person spends a considerable amount of time working, dedicating 92,000 hours over the course of their lives. Society often associates work with negativity, but there's a whole world waiting to be explored, filled with people to meet, opportunities to seize and memories to create that will last a lifetime. Don't limit yourself or let fear prevent you from seeking out these experiences and opportunities for fun. While work can offer valuable lessons and experiences, leisure can bring balance and rejuvenation.

Working and finding balance in our lives is crucial for our growth and development. While working is necessary for survival, it is important to find a job that allows us to enhance our skills and brings us satisfaction. It is possible to maintain a positive outlook on life even in difficult situations. Our work extends beyond our careers, and we must also prioritise our health, our home environment and our relationships with loved ones. Relying on others to bring about a positive change in our lives is not the solution. It is up to each individual to create the life they want. As the saying goes, "If you want something done, you've got to do it yourself." This is especially true when it comes to personal growth and fulfilment. Ultimately, only you truly know what you want, and it's up to you to make it happen. While it can be tempting to rely on others for a positive change in your life, it's important to remember that you are ultimately responsible for your own well-being and growth. Our belief systems can have a significant impact on our motivation and drive. For those with religious faith, seeking guidance from a higher power can provide strength and direction. However, it's important to regularly examine and refine our beliefs to ensure they align with and support our personal goals. As a Christian, my belief system guides me to listen to where God is directing me, and in His strength, I am able to achieve my goals. The sense of accomplishment that comes from hard work and personal growth is priceless, more so when it aligns with one's belief system. Although work is inevitable, we can make the most of it by focusing on meaningful efforts that contribute to our growth and development. By prioritising self-improvement, we can become the best versions of ourselves.

7.6. REALISATIONS

We don't always have the answers, even when we believe we do. I've witnessed many individuals try to tackle challenges based on their prior knowledge and experience or by hoping for a miraculous outcome.

Unfortunately, this approach doesn't always work. The world is constantly changing, and it's essential to keep up with these changes. This is a valuable lesson that I've learned through difficult experiences. Although discovering this truth can be disheartening, it helps us grow and strengthens us to handle similar struggles in the future. I once attended a workshop on emotional well-being, mental health and spiritual healing hosted by Teal Swan. The session was interactive, and the participants were invited to share their experiences. One significant memory of the workshop was when a person came to the stage to talk about their struggles in a long-term relationship. During the discussion, Teal delved into the reasons and dynamics of the situation. To my surprise, the person wanted to resolve the conflict, but was held back by anxiety and fear of taking the necessary steps towards it. They had convinced themselves that if they continued with the same approach, things would eventually change. This experience highlights the importance of going beyond our understanding and breaking out of our comfort zones. We can't rely solely on past experiences and knowledge to solve problems. Instead, we need to venture into the unknown with an open mind and willingness to learn and grow. Our past is behind us and may not serve us in the present or future. It's crucial not to let past experiences dictate our future experiences. We have the power to create new paths and break away from the cycle of repeating the same patterns.

Throughout my life, I have faced many challenges, setbacks, and obstacles. Each time, I learnt something new or realised that some of the things I was doing, even though I thought they were helpful, were actually obstacles. To share an example, I used to frequently isolate myself from social situations due to my fear of being judged or rejected. I used to pretend that I was busy and distract myself with materialistic activities, but deep down, I knew that true happiness came from connecting with others. Realising that I was trying to distract myself from the fear of how people would perceive me, I made an effort to balance my social and personal time. This way, I could still enjoy my hobbies while also spending time with others and forming the connections I needed. These were truths I didn't want to acknowledge, but ignoring them would have trapped me in a never-ending cycle of sadness.

I had to be open-minded and ready to embrace the unknown realities of life. Reading books was a key tool in helping me gain new perspectives and shift my mind-set. During the pandemic, I felt like I had to forget everything I thought I knew about the world, and embrace new lessons. By not letting past experiences dictate my understanding, I was able to uncover a range of new insights that made sense in terms of what we all want, need and search for in life. These new insights align with what is considered to be the universal desires and experiences of humanity. It seems that these lessons tap into the fundamental nature of human beings and what we all yearn for, need and search for. I found myself having many "Aha!" moments when everything suddenly made sense. In addition to reading books, watching films and TV shows also taught me important life lessons. Don't be afraid to ask questions or seek answers, even if they seem odd or unconventional. The satisfaction of finding the answers is worth it. As you navigate through life, take the time to seek truth and love. Don't feel pressured to have all the answers, as that is an unrealistic expectation. Explore your own mind and the world around you, and you'll be surprised by the wisdom you'll uncover, as long as you keep an open mind. This is your life, and you should live it to the fullest, without letting anyone hold you back. Embrace new experiences and strive for the biggest victories, making each one count. To end, let me quote a memorable line from the film "Titanic.":

Life is a gift, don't intend on wasting it. You never know what hand you're going to get dealt next. You'll learn to take life as it comes at you... to make each day count.

(Titanic, 1997)

08. When in Doubt

8.1. WONDERING

Doubts can seep into our minds at any moment. Whether we're working, socialising, making significant life decisions or investing in relationships, doubt can be a weighty distraction that throws us off course. It is especially challenging to deal with when we're on the fast track to achieving our dreams. The most damaging thing about doubt is how it chips away at our confidence, making us question who we are and what we're doing.

As we work towards our goals, we may occasionally pause to contemplate the potential outcomes that may or may not come to fruition. The outcomes of our decisions are often unpredictable. Some of us may take time to think about ourselves, our lives, the events that unfold and the kind of person we aspire to be. For those who are constantly engrossed in their work without taking a break, there may be a question of whether they stop to reflect on the direction their life is taking. The weight of the world on our shoulders is often underestimated, and this may lead to conflicting situations, particularly when we're deciding what we want to do or how we want to behave in this world. There may be times when people try to control our thoughts, telling us what to do and what to like, and even insulting us if we have different preferences. This can create several conflicting beliefs, which can cause us to doubt our choices. Sometimes, it may seem easier to go with the flow, believing that everything will fall into place, but it is essential to ask ourselves if we are truly happy. As we navigate our lives, doubts and uncertainties may arise. Our choices can be influenced by external factors, which may lead us to question our beliefs. The key is to remain true to ourselves and ask ourselves the essential questions that matter to our happiness and well-being. Only through self-reflection and honesty can we find our true direction in life.

How often do you question whether you're headed in the right direction in life? Do you wonder if you're in the right job, relationships or place? Have you ever felt stuck in a loop, wondering whether you should break free and try something new? Have you ever doubted your decisions or felt lost and confused? Only you know your life better than anyone else, so the best person to provide you with the answers to these questions is yourself. If you aren't sure of the motivations behind your choices, it's worth digging deeper to find out. Making decisions without reason or purpose can leave you feeling unfulfilled. Don't make decisions for others' happiness or validation, as it's impossible to please everyone. This approach can lead to burnout, self-doubt and a lack of self-worth. Instead, prioritise your growth and stay in tune with your desires and values. By focusing on what truly matters to you, you can break free from the cycle of uncertainty and find a greater sense of purpose and identity.

Life is a complex subject that can be overwhelming to contemplate. It's tempting to just stick to our routines and follow the crowd, but is that really what we want? At some point, we may find ourselves wondering how we got to where we are and whether we're on the right path. This kind of introspection is not a sign of weakness or embarrassment; in fact, it's essential for figuring out what we truly want out of life. While you may have insignificant fleeting thoughts like wondering if it will be warm tomorrow or if your favourite cookies will be in stock at the store, deep introspection about your life can help you discover what you truly desire in life. Take the time to be honest with yourself and use logic to uncover your true purpose and direction.

8.2. SUDDEN CHANGES IN YOUR LIFE

Change is an inevitable part of life, and it can be either welcomed or resisted. What comes to your mind when you think of sudden changes? Did your perception of certain people change? Did your beliefs or opinions about something change? These changes can feel surreal, especially when they involve people leaving us or changing in ways that make them less familiar to us. When someone we thought was a close friend becomes distant or starts treating us poorly, doubts about the depth of our relationship can creep in. We may wonder if they ever really cared about us at all.

Have you ever doubted your decisions in life, whether in your career or personal goals? Doubt is a common feeling when things don't go as planned. It reminds us that no matter how much we try to control our lives, unexpected circumstances can throw us off course. It's a tough pill to swallow, but when we accept that change is inevitable, it becomes a little easier to deal with. When life takes an unexpected turn, it's important to process your feelings, but not let them consume you. Make room in your mind for courage and confidence to seize the next opportunity. As the saying goes, "if at first you don't succeed, try again." Our doubts can often be rooted in past experiences that didn't go as planned, causing us to believe that similar situations will have similar outcomes. This applies not only to our lives but also to the lives of those who seek our advice when they find themselves in similar circumstances. In more extreme situations like losing a loved one, being made redundant or facing a global pandemic, questions and doubts can feel overwhelming. Such circumstances can cause us to question the trajectory of our lives, and make us wonder if our lives will ever get better again.

When sudden roadblocks arise and intense emotions surface, it's important to acknowledge that your emotions are valid. Take time to process your feelings in a healthy way, even if others try to invalidate them. I'm sorry for any hardships you may have faced and want to acknowledge the difficulty of processing sudden shocks. Remove any negative thoughts that may cause you to doubt your ability if a similar situation should arise. Remember that your past doesn't have to define your future. Each day brings new opportunities for growth, and while it may be tempting to let fear hold you back, taking a leap of faith can be a powerful step forward. To overcome doubts, you must ignore the obstacles that stand in your way. This is a sign of your resilience. Believe that you are capable of achieving anything you set your mind to, and don't let anyone else make you believe otherwise. It's better to try and fail than to never try at all. Change is often scary because, as humans, we prefer familiarity, but change can also be an opportunity for growth and positive transformation.

8.3. WHAT IF?

Have you ever felt like the grass would be greener on the other side? It's that feeling of wanting more or wishing for greater happiness. Wishing is something we do regularly, especially when we're going through a difficult situation. We often wish we could rub a lamp and a genie would appear to grant us unlimited wishes. Unfortunately, wishes don't come true instantly just by lounging in a chair and raising our fingers. Any desired outcome will require effort.

There are times when we find ourselves in dark situations, such as when we are subjected to abuse or oppression, when we face rejection, when we feel like the world is against us or when well-planned endeavours fail. These can be painful and lonely experiences that make us cry out to God (Even those who don't believe in God may find themselves doing so). However, we should not feel defeated, as there are always opportunities for our lives to turn around. By adopting the right mind-set, we can overcome our struggles and remind ourselves that we're doing our best. While it may be challenging to find a way out of the darkness, it's important to remember that there is always light at the end of the tunnel. It's understandable to dwell on the past and wonder what could have been, but it's essential not to get stuck in that mind-set. Instead, focus your energy on creating the life you want for yourself. Don't let your doubts and fears prevent you from moving forward. You are capable of achieving your goals, and with determination and effort, you can find the light that leads you out of the darkness.

Merely daydreaming about living a different life provides only temporary satisfaction. This realisation dawned on me when I found myself wishing for a life other than the one I currently have. If I wanted long-term satisfaction, I needed to consider how to make my wishes a reality. This involved reflecting on my career, New Year's resolutions, the possessions and projects I desired and the ways to become a better version of myself. It can be daunting to think about all the necessary steps and hard work involved in achieving our goals, but my faith in God as a Christian, gave me strength and perseverance. The Bible verse, "Do not be anxious about anything, but in every situation, by prayer and petition, with thanksgiving, present your requests to God." (The Bible - Philippians 4:6), has provided me with comfort and guidance. I've been amazed by how God has answered my prayers, although not always in the way I initially expected. As a believer, I understand that I shouldn't pray with selfish ambition or vain deceit (The Bible - Philippians 2:3), as those kinds of prayers are often not answered. Of course, I recognise that this perspective may not resonate with everyone. Along with my faith, the support of my friends has also been instrumental in helping me take the necessary steps to achieve my goals. I've learned that having a good support system, combined with my inner strength can help make my dreams a reality and eliminate any self-doubt when working towards a goal. I wholeheartedly believe that where we put our efforts is a reflection of where our heart is truly focused.

8.4. BODY IMAGE AND SELF-ACCEPTANCE

The decision to alter one's physical appearance through cosmetic surgery can be a sensitive topic. However, it raises important questions about our self-perception.

While there could be multiple reasons why people desire to alter their physical appearance, the underlying concern is often their perception that their natural selves are not good enough. When we seek to change a part of our body due to dissatisfaction or to emulate someone else, it often stems from a feeling of dislike towards our authentic selves. However, I firmly believe that we can learn to appreciate and love all of our original features. I also guarantee that there are many others who will love the original parts of who you are, despite any criticism you may have experienced. We need to appreciate our unique beauty and accept ourselves for who we are.

I want to make it clear that I am not opposed to plastic surgery when it is used to save lives or correct medical conditions. However, I believe that undergoing surgery with the intention of significantly altering our appearance solely to conform to society's standards or to be more attractive to others is not a healthy practise. The promotion of cosmetic surgery only serves to boost the profits of the industry, enabling it to expand and exert greater influence over more regions of the world. Moreover, it may propagate the false message that altering one's physical appearance is key to achieving happiness or gaining affection. For those who have undergone surgery to alter their bodies, it is important to remember that they still have the option to keep their original body parts. It is possible to be loved and accepted for who they are, regardless of any physical changes they may have made. It's helpful to remember that our feelings are fleeting, and this includes the desire to change our physical appearance in order to feel more loved. As much as we may want to act on our feelings, changing an original part of our body for something new will not bring the contentment we seek. This is especially true when our initial desire to change ourselves fades away. The deep-seated feeling is not a desire to alter your appearance but rather a longing for acceptance of your true self. I can assure you that it is possible to be loved for who you are. We should never doubt our originality, as this is how we were created to be. Embrace the natural evolution of your life journey, rather than trying to force changes through cosmetic procedures. Let's start loving the body and skin we're in, and if anyone tells us otherwise, let's confidently reject their standards and celebrate our unique selves.

8.5. REFER BACK TO YOUR BELIEFS

When we begin to doubt a situation, person or place we're about to enter, a myriad of questions may arise in our minds, making it difficult to think straight. First, you need to take time to relax yourself. Identify the most effective method for you to achieve this as your mind is unable to function effectively while in a state of panic or "fight-or-flight" response. During such times, the body is focused on either fighting or running away. There are several methods that can help you relax, or in other words, practise mindfulness. During my time at the Empath Academy, I learnt that being mindful entails being present in the moment without allowing intrusive thoughts triggering extreme emotions. Depending on the environment you're in, some methods may be more effective than others.

Some methods I find particularly helpful to me include steady breathing, the use of the five senses and excessive movement or exercise. Ecstatic dancing is particularly effective for me. Playing any song that encourages movement and getting my body in motion clears my head. Walking and connecting with nature also has a similar effect on me. For example, in situations where I couldn't leave the room, steady breathing kept my mind stable. There are different breathing patterns, each of which works differently for different people. It's essential to find a comfortable method that suits each situation and ensures that we do not cause any harm to ourselves or others. Using harmful methods like damaging objects or engaging in self-harm is not a healthy way to deal with anxiety.

Have you ever encountered people who say one thing but do the opposite? For instance, someone might declare that drugs are harmful, yet have a drug addiction. Or they might acknowledge that their partner is abusive, yet choose to remain in the relationship. This kind of behaviour creates a disconnect between what people say and what they do, and it's known as cognitive dissonance. Deep down, people know that hurting others is wrong and that self-sabotage and substance abuse can lead to destructive cycles that distance us from the things and people we love. However, humans tend to cling to what's familiar, even if it's unhealthy or harmful. If someone has been in a neglectful relationship for a long time, they might become so accustomed to the mistreatment that they feel more comfortable in that situation than in a new, healthier relationship. The thought of leaving the familiar, even if it's unhealthy and venturing into the unknown can be terrifying. Facing the truth and moving on, can be an emotional challenge, as it threatens to uproot our sense of security and stability. Once you've processed your emotions and are in a clear state of mind, use the knowledge and logic you possess to carefully and healthily navigate the situation. Feeding our minds with the right information and logic can help us face any challenge with courage. Our minds can be programmed to follow a default thought pattern, depending on what we regularly reflect and meditate on.

In our infancy, our minds are blank slates, and we learn based on the environment our parents provide for us and how they teach us. Videos of toddlers imitating their parent's actions and movements demonstrate how we absorb everything we are exposed to during childhood. We can't learn things we aren't aware of; it all comes from our environment. Unfortunately, children growing up in an environment where yelling, mistreatment and physical abuse are prevalent are likely to pick up these negative behaviours and use them when they interact with the outside world. Without being taught kindness, humility and courtesy, the child is likely to default to regular aggression and continue the cycle.

However, it doesn't have to be a permanent situation. When a child grows up and becomes an adult, they have the opportunity to create their own space outside of their parents' home and learn new behaviours through reading, observing and meditating. Meditating and reflecting on constructive thoughts and beliefs that reinforce your self-worth can help you avoid negative thoughts and feelings that undermine your confidence and make you feel like you cannot be accepted for who you truly are.

Example statements to meditate could be “I am worthy of love”, “There is someone who accepts me for who I am” and “I possess unique talents and traits”. Consistently engaging in healthy, constructive, peaceful, delicate and loving behaviour can help individuals overcome any aggressive behaviour they may have been taught (or have learnt) as children. As time passes, these new beliefs can take root and guide their actions in dealing with situations, allowing them to trust and act on their inner thoughts and feelings more easily. While it’s perfectly fine to seek advice from others when feeling lost, having a solid belief system provides a clear direction on how to view life and everything around us.

Those who practise different religions may find their own ways to achieve inner peace by referring to the teachings of their congregations and communities. I understand that the concept of worshipping a god may not appeal to everyone, as it may seem like we’re giving up our true selves to become someone that God wants us to be. However, as a long-term Christian, I can confidently say that God has not controlled me over the years. Instead, my faith has helped me connect with my true self more than any other person has. It was through my faith that I found direction and purpose in life, which I hold onto tightly. It gives me a reason to get out of bed in the morning and to work and love to the best of my ability. My faith constantly assures me that even when I am rejected by the world, God will accept me, for I am fearfully and wonderfully made in His image (The Bible - Psalm 139:14).

8.6. WHAT OR WHO DO YOU LISTEN TO?

At times, we may not realise that the decisions we make in life are not truly our own. Growing up in an environment with strict discipline or being surrounded by controlling individuals can lead to a mental state where we prioritise meeting other people's needs over our own. Sometimes, we may fear rejection and seek validation, which can make us hesitant to express ourselves confidently. The fear of being criticised can prevent us from pursuing things that could benefit us. As someone who has experienced the feeling of being trapped in different aspects of life, I understand the impact that this mind-set can have on personal growth and success. Even when we watch others make choices that don't make sense and appear to be moving forward slowly, they can still surprise us at the last moment.

People who start businesses and experience a few failures before achieving success have surely faced doubts from others, and possibly themselves. But when perseverance, courage and passion all come into play, the comments from haters and doubters feel insignificant. It's inevitable that people around us may disagree with our life choices and discourage us with comments like, "you're not good enough," "you don't have the skills" and "you're going to suffer severely." But if you believe in yourself and put in the work, you don't have to let their words pull you away from your goals, especially if they don't know your story.

Passion, courage and perseverance are essential traits that can help us achieve our goals and overcome challenges, both in our personal and professional lives. These traits are interrelated, and their combination can lead to great success. Passion is a potent driving force that stems from genuine interest and excitement in a particular activity or goal. When we are passionate about something, we are more likely to succeed because we are motivated by our intrinsic desires rather than external pressure.

Courage is another vital trait that reveals one's strength and willingness to face daunting challenges to attain a goal. It is not the absence of fear but the ability to overcome it. This can be seen in the determination of superheroes in action films who confront their fears to defeat their adversaries.

Perseverance is the act of persisting through challenges and setbacks, even when it feels like we have hit a dead-end. It involves focusing on our end goal, breaking down large tasks into smaller, achievable steps and staying committed to the process. By not focusing on the tiredness of the journey but instead on the end goal, we are more likely to make progress and achieve success. For example, marathon runners may experience physical pain and exhaustion, but they endure and reach the finish line. Similarly, businesses may face delays and setbacks, but with a dedicated team focused on delivering a successful project, the feeling of triumph is akin to receiving a trophy. As an engineer, I have experienced this feeling not only at work but also in small home projects. My home improvement projects have evolved over the years. They started off as paintings and drawings that allowed me to bring my illustration ideas to life, and it was gratifying to witness an idea in my mind materialise into reality. The projects transformed into crafting activities. I began constructing Airfix model kits and eventually gained the confidence to build models from scratch. Some of my favourite projects are those that I have built from scratch, such as film props and costumes, and I like to keep them on display to remind myself of how much my skills have developed over time.

I believe that practising the three traits - passion, courage and perseverance - can not only help you embrace your authentic self but also protect you from naysayers who don't share your views. However, it's important not to resort to ruthless tactics to achieve your goals. Becoming someone who tramples over others to get what they want is not the way to go. Though others may try to impede your progress, don't stoop to their level. You don't want to become your own worst enemy. When you're in touch with your true self, what's meant for you will come to you naturally, and you won't have to fight anyone to attain it. It's been passion, courage and perseverance that have inspired me to write this book. I had many doubts that I wouldn't be able to write a book because I wasn't good at English. Thanks to the encouragement of my closest friends, I was motivated to start writing about the things that had helped me in my healing journey. As I began to write more about my experiences and the lessons I had learned, I soon had enough content to create a book. I am sharing this with you to encourage you not to doubt your abilities. I had doubts about writing a book, but I ended up writing this very book. I know you can overcome the obstacle of doubt and achieve anything you set your mind to. It's important to take the time to discover your calling in life by spending time alone and exploring your interests. We spend thousands of hours working in our lives, so finding a job that brings us joy can make the pain of work much more bearable. Your passions may change over time, and that's okay. Through our experiences, we gain a better understanding of the direction we want to take in life. It's important to find your calling and pursue it; don't let others discourage you. It's easy to follow society's expectations to fit in, but the real question is: Are you truly happy with yourself? Do you genuinely enjoy what you're doing now? Do you want to try something new? Are you simply going with the flow because everyone else is, or are you pursuing your true passions?

8.7. KEEP WATCH

Doubts can creep up on us at unexpected times and can be triggered at various circumstances. It can cause us to doubt our relationships, actions, jobs and abilities. Doubting ourselves can be a troubling feeling as we progress through life and strive to achieve our goals. When negative thoughts arise and try to steer us away from believing in ourselves, it's important to take notice of where these voices may be coming from. Perhaps a similar situation in the past made us feel doubtful, but it's important to remember that the past does not dictate the present. Remind yourself of your abilities, gifts and the opportunities that lie ahead. Never let doubt limit how far you can go because every day is a new chance to try again. Letting even the smallest amount of doubt seep into your mind is like giving your enemy a foothold.

Remember the saying "never give an inch" and apply it when doubts arise. Doubts can be triggered by a range of situations, including when situations change from good to bad. In some cases, they may indicate a need to distance oneself from the situation to preserve one's health and well-being. Alternatively, doubts can stem from feelings of inadequacy, whether it's a belief that one is not good enough to achieve a particular goal or that one lacks the ability to help others effectively.

In a situation where you feel that a person or situation is not keeping up with their words or you don't know what to expect from them, doubt can be a useful tool to help you recognise the reality of the situation. For example, if you have a relationship that has changed over time and a person becomes less reliable, a feeling of doubt could show us that we may need to reduce how much we can depend on them. We don't need to lose all of our trust in them right away; instead, gradually increase your trust in them based on how much they deliver. That way, you can be less doubtful of them because you know what to expect from them. When dealing with a person who you can't completely trust, you don't have to believe them if you don't feel completely comfortable with them. We can choose what we put our beliefs and faith in, but in doing so; we need to be in a peaceful mind-set.

The other type of doubt, in which you feel inferior or like a failure, is called toxic doubt, which can hinder your progress. If you encounter negative comments from pessimistic people, it's best to avoid internalising their words, as they do not know you as well as you do. Instead, stay strong in your beliefs and values, and give yourself the comfort, grace and kindness you need to take big steps and pursue your passions. When you step out of your comfort zone to take on new challenges and pursue your goals, it's crucial to recognise and give yourself credit for the courage and effort you've put in. We tend to get comfortable with familiarity, but taking risks can lead to significant accomplishments and personal growth.

You can achieve anything you set your mind to and stay true to yourself, even when people try to convince you otherwise. By meditating on positive beliefs about yourself, you can reduce the amount of toxic doubt that others may try to impose upon you. Even if things don't always go your way, know that you have another opportunity waiting for you. Don't let doubt be a stumbling block in your life. Keep searching for opportunities and reminding yourself of who you are and what you are capable of. Pay attention to the different types of doubt you may experience. When doubt is filled with fear, anxiety, and depression, it can be toxic and may be attacking you. In contrast, doubt that calmly warns you of a threatening situation can guide you safely. Believe in yourself and your abilities, and strive to be the best version of yourself that you can be.

09. Even When Alone

9.1. ALONE TIME

How does the thought of being alone make you feel? I've noticed that people have mixed feelings about this, at least based on what I see on social media. On one hand, I see plenty of profiles that showcase people surrounded by loved ones and lots of comments about how great it is to be around others. On the other hand, there are also plenty of comments about how annoying people can be, and how some people prefer to be alone. I've read comments like "All I need in life is a big comfy bed, snacks and a big TV in my room" or "I need my space," and so on.

I believe that we definitely need to have some alone time in our lives. It allows us to clear our minds from the world's pressures, reflect on our thoughts and develop plans for our future. Whether we use our moments of solitude constructively or simply to unwind, it can be a much-needed break from the voices and demands of others. However, no human was meant to be alone forever. People who are isolated in prison cells for long periods are likely to have suffered psychologically from a lack of social interaction. Therefore, while moments of solitude can be healthy and helpful, it's important to also nurture our relationships with others. In today's fast-paced world, we often feel pressured to tend to the needs of others, and as a result, we neglect to take care of ourselves. Since we are the ones who know our priorities best, it's important to recognise when we need alone time and to schedule it into our routines. While it's natural to want to spend time with our loved ones, we also need to take care of ourselves before we reach a state of burnout.

Don't be afraid to communicate to those around you that you need alone time when you need it. If someone criticises or ostracises you for wanting alone time after working hard, then you don't need to listen to them. Remember to give yourself grace and comfort, and make time for self-care. Your support circle needs to understand that you need time to re-energise and take care of yourself, no matter what your situation is. Whether you're a parent, a professional, a worker or someone who works a lot, you still need time to replenish your health. Your support circle will understand that just like everyone else, you too need some alone time to take care of yourself. They should recognise all of your needs and help fulfil them. Your alone time can completely refuel your body and mind, and it can help you discover or remind yourself of your interests, life direction and inner happiness.

When I have some alone time, I like to explore the hobbies and interests that I've practised throughout my life. Engaging in these activities has allowed me to flourish and grow in my passions. Some of my favourite hobbies include painting, drawing, crafting, cosplaying, watching films, going for walks, reading and listening to online sermons. During the COVID-19 lockdown, I decided to take on a new challenge and started making multiple Iron Man suit costumes, which I planned to showcase at comic conventions once the COVID restrictions were lifted. These projects kept me busy while I had to stay indoors, and as a huge Marvel fan and full-time engineer, I felt that my passion for cosplaying allowed me to express a part of my personality that might not have been obvious in my day-to-day work.

After enjoying my alone time, I often feel ready to reconnect with the world around me. Whether it's by calling or messaging my closest friends through social media or attending church or social events, I make sure to engage in activities that provide the interaction I need. While it can be challenging to strike the perfect balance, taking the time to get to know yourself during moments of solitude can greatly enhance your ability to connect and re-energise.

9.2. FEELING LONELY

Although alone time can be refreshing, too much of it can leave us feeling disheartened and lonely. We, humans, are social creatures, and we need to interact with others to survive. There may be moments when you try to connect with the people you love, but they may be unavailable due to their own priorities. This can leave you feeling lonely, especially when you see others surrounded by their family, friends, life partners or support circles. While it can be difficult when the people we love are unavailable, it's important to take care of ourselves and find ways to build ourselves up during these moments of loneliness. Whether it's through treating ourselves to something special or practising self-care, we need to remember that we deserve the same care and attention we give to others. It's often said, "Feel free to reach out to me anytime", but for those struggling with deep loneliness and depression, it can be mentally draining to muster the energy to reach out for help. They may need someone who can show them that their pain is being acknowledged. For those who are fortunate enough to have a solid support system, I encourage you to think about those who may not. Do you know anyone who is alone, isolated or doesn't have their own family or partner? Consider reaching out to them through a call or a random message. Sometimes, all it takes is a little gesture of kindness to pull someone out of loneliness.

There may be children who are suffering from abuse whilst living with their parents, as well as single individuals who feel like no one is reaching out to them or noticing their difficult situations. I understand that life can get busy, but it is important to make time to help those who may be on the verge of self-harm. Not everyone has the same level of access to love and support, and taking the time to reach out to those who are lacking it can help us distribute love more evenly in the world. We should strive to create a world where everyone feels loved and cared for, but to do so, we need to start by noticing those who are lonely and showing them that they matter.

In any relationship, it is important to strike a balance between time spent with the other person for the intimacy to grow, and alone time for us to individually replenish our health. When we reach out to the lonely, they will feel more loved and energised, which enables them to communicate better with others. Have you ever seen someone who is heavily depressed or drained from lack of love, to the point that they retreat to an isolated place and shut the world out as a way to cope with their pain? Experiencing trauma can often result in the development of coping mechanisms as a way to manage the pain that comes with rejection or being ignored. When individuals have no one to confide in or share their feelings with, they may express those feelings in unconventional ways. Some individuals may even inflict pain on themselves as a way to reduce the impact of pain caused by others. When people lack the appropriate resources to safely release their pain, they may resort to reckless or extreme measures to outwardly express their inner feelings.

To give a few examples, individuals may become verbally or physically aggressive, develop substance addictions that lead to significant financial expenditures, or become co-dependent on a habit or material possession. They may even threaten anyone who attempts to take it away from them, even if it is for their own well-being. They may even become less aware of their destructive habits because if they see them as their only source of comfort, they will be less aware of how much harm they cause themselves and others. These people must receive recognition and love, to make them feel like their existence is appreciated. When we examine the world around us, it becomes apparent that some individuals receive more love, attention and recognition than others. If you are fortunate enough to have a strong support system, it is important to remain mindful of those who may not have such a network. Consider reaching out to these individuals and offering them support and companionship. On the other hand, if you find yourself feeling lonely and isolated, it is important to prioritise your own well-being and seek out activities and hobbies that bring you joy. Remember to be kind and gentle with yourself, and don't hesitate to ask for help when you need it. It's natural to feel discouraged at times, but try to hold on to the belief that there are people who will appreciate and value you for who you are.

9.3. THE INNER CHILD

During my trauma healing course at the Empath Academy, I participated in a course called "Learn to Love Yourself." It was a short yet powerful course that allowed me to reconnect with the lighter aspects of myself that I felt were not valued by the people in my life. It was during this course that I first learnt about the concept of the inner child. The inner child is an essential part of our personality that remains with us even as we grow older, carrying all the lessons, experiences and interests we learnt during childhood. It encompasses all the little memories, songs, games, media and joys we found as children, which later becomes the foundation for our adulthood. As we grow older, it's our responsibility to become self-sustaining, but there are still interests and thoughts from our childhood that we carry with us. Some of us recognise and continue to care for our inner child, while others may ignore it and move on with their lives. Our inner child carries not only the positive experiences but also the negative ones. Childhood trauma can follow us into adulthood, and the behaviour and beliefs we exhibit may reveal what we didn't receive as children.

Everyone has likely experienced some kind of trauma as a child, especially during the stage where we make mistakes and disobey our parents. We may have thrown temper tantrums when things were taken away from us or when we were severely punished or bullied. These experiences could have made us feel inadequate, unlovable and incompetent. Without thinking too hard, I'm sure you can recall moments from your past where you experienced intense emotions. Our childhood experiences shape us in profound ways, and while some of these experiences are positive, others can be traumatic. These early experiences can impact us as adults, particularly if we have not received the support we needed as children. This can either a lack of emotional recognition, physical nurturing or basic material needs. We all have certain needs, and these needs cannot be ignored or "unneeded". Our basic needs for things like oxygen, water and nourishment are essential, but so are our emotional needs for recognition, support and guidance. If these needs were not met when we were children, we may continue to suffer from the effects of this deficit in our adulthood.

As adults, we may benefit from looking back and acknowledging the needs of our inner child. Some people may believe that they do not have the time to focus on their inner child, or they may avoid revisiting their traumatic childhood experiences altogether. I understand the fear and reluctance to do so, as I have been in that position myself. However, unhealed trauma can manifest in physical and emotional ways; our bodies require nurturing and healing. While it may be scary to revisit traumatic events from the past, it is important to address any pain that may still be present. In the same way that we would care for a physical wound, we must take care of our emotional wounds. Trauma may not always be visible like a physical scar, but it can be just as real and impactful. It is a wound in the mind that needs attention and care. I was taught by my coach at the Empath Academy that it is not necessary to relive childhood trauma to heal from it. Rather, we can begin by acknowledging and recognising the inner wounds that we carry with us. I encourage you to take the time to reflect on your own experiences and discover the strength that comes from healing your inner child. If you know you experienced difficult times as a child, prioritising your own healing and growth can lead to a more fulfilling life. When making time for yourself to work on healing your inner child, it's important to balance having fun and self-improvement. Identifying the root cause of any unresolved issues can lead to complete resolution. Don't let fear or lack of awareness hold you back from healing old wounds. Ignoring trauma is like leaving a splinter in your arm - it may be painful to remove, but once it's out, you can fully heal and move on. Your inner child will always be a part of you, so it's worth taking the time to nurture and give them the attention they may have lacked in the past. Reconnecting with your inner child can be both enjoyable and healing. In the following section, I will provide tips to help you connect with your inner child.

9.4. RECONNECTING WITH THE INNER CHILD

I had a lot of fun connecting with my inner child for the first time through the "Learn to Love Yourself" course. The course was initially referred to as "inner child work," but I found it more approachable when it was rephrased as "inner child play." As an artist, I found that the activities involving drawing and colouring were especially effective in quickly transporting me to the childlike mind-set I needed to connect with. For the course homework, I drew myself surrounded by all the positive things I remembered from my childhood, such as video games, songs, films, drawings and favourite meals.

Favourite Artists from childhood:

- Lighthouse Family
- Blue
- S Club 7
- Britney Spears
- Busted
- Michael Jackson
- Spice Girls
- Abba

Favourite Films and TV Shows from childhood:

- Toy Story
- A Bug's Life
- Chicken Run
- The Lion King
- Thunderbirds
- George of the Jungle
- Thomas the Tank Engine
- Lilo and Stitch

Overall, I found the language used in the course to be clear and easy to understand, which made the experience even more enjoyable. I hope my examples sparked some fond memories for you as well. When I was reminded of all the positive experiences from my past, I began to appreciate that my inner child is just as alive today as it was back then. This realisation helped me understand what my inner child required to heal from past trauma and pain. Fortunately, as an adult, I was able to provide my inner child with what it needed. As strange as it may seem at first, you can parent your own inner child when you come of age. As you become comfortable with the process, it can actually be quite enjoyable. Connecting with your inner child requires setting aside dedicated time, and it's important not to let others make you feel guilty for doing so. Everyone needs to connect with their inner child every now and then to keep that youthful spark alive as we get older. In our society, getting older is often seen as a negative thing. But it's important to remember that ageing is inevitable and not necessarily a bad thing. Staying connected with your inner child can help you maintain a youthful perspective and prevent you from feeling old.

For those who have had a challenging childhood and may struggle to recall happy memories, I want you to know that I see you and offer my heartfelt support. I encourage you to get in touch with your inner child and you can start by identifying what your inner child needs and taking the necessary action to fulfil those needs. Don't worry about how it may appear to others; this is about taking care of yourself and finding comfort. If there was something you longed for in childhood but didn't receive, consider ways to fulfil that desire for yourself. If you're looking to reconnect with your inner child, take some time to reflect on what brings you excitement and joy, and let those feelings flourish. Just think about how babies and toddlers approach life - they don't know anything about criticism, insults, racism, sexism, war, popularity or any of the things that divide us as humans. Only when elders impose divisive beliefs and behaviour do children learn to judge based on appearances or actions. As we grow older, we may lose touch with this carefree spirit, but it's never too late to reclaim it. Try to tap into the positive memories of your childhood and make time to engage in playful activities that bring you joy. We all need to nurture our inner child and cultivate a sense of playfulness in our lives.

9.5. LIFE DIRECTION

Life presents us with many choices, and some of them can be especially challenging. When we have the voices of others clamouring in our minds, we may find it difficult to hear our own thoughts, much less make a clear decision. Even if we manage to quiet those external voices, we will inevitably encounter difficult and stressful situations. Some choices may not have a clear-cut right or wrong answer, while others may have serious consequences if we make the wrong decision. Regardless, we always have the power to choose. Life presents us with numerous options and crossroads, be it in our relationships, career, beliefs, passions or unexpected events. No matter what direction we take, we all desire the same things - happiness, safety and love. We also want to feel significant and valued in all aspects of our lives.

A vital ingredient for a satisfying life is discovering our purpose. Some people may not prioritise finding their purpose and just live life as it comes, enjoying the moment. However, it's crucial to note that living without purpose can cause harm. Purpose refers to the reason for someone or something to exist, and if you're reading this book, you have a reason to exist. You're alive, you're present and you've undoubtedly impacted someone's life. Believing that you lack purpose can lead to feelings of insignificance, emptiness and depression. You may not agree with me right now, but if you're reading this, you have a life, which means you have a purpose. I encourage you to start believing that you have a purpose in life, and that belief can positively drive you towards a happier and more fulfilled life. When I was growing up and contemplating my aspirations in life, I was also dealing with my own trauma. I dreamt endlessly about a life in which I was in a much happier place, and all the trauma I had faced was a distant memory. While my reality isn't exactly what I had envisioned, that doesn't necessarily make it bad. I envisioned myself being surrounded by a supportive circle of people who loved me for who I am, having the job I had always desired, achieving my goals and going on the most amazing adventures. I can confidently say that I am doing a lot of what I had dreamt of, and it feels great. However, this didn't just happen on its own; I had to make it happen. Even during times when I felt depressed from losing friends or finding my work life difficult, my dreams encouraged me to look forward to my future and the life that I could create.

A concept that consumed me for years, yet I had no name for it until I read the book "Adult Children of Emotionally Immature Parents", was the idea that my countless hours of watching films and TV shows, combined with my vivid dreams of a happier life, formed elaborate stories where my pain was healed and I found eternal happiness. According to the book, these fantasies of a better life are experienced by children who have experienced severe trauma and loneliness. They are called healing fantasies, and they involve imagining a life where we finally get what we've always needed or lacked in childhood. I once thought that this concept was unique to me, but upon reading the book, I realised that many others have experienced similar fantasies. This concept is shown in the Marvel TV show "WandaVision" (2021). These fantasies can linger in our minds for a long time, and at times we can become too attached to them. Such attachment can lead to the formation of expectations of those around us, and we may become angry or upset if they fail to match what we imagined in our fantasy. While healing fantasies can motivate us to create the life we desire, it is important not to become obsessed with them to the point of becoming irrational. When we start yelling or getting mad at people for not meeting our expectations, it is a sign of severe attachment to our fantasies. It's essential to come back to reality to avoid being too absorbed in our own thoughts. Dreams and fantasies can bring us happiness and direction, but if we get too attached, we can lose touch with reality, leading to feelings of gloominess. For those who don't dream as much, interacting with the world can help you determine the direction you want to take in life.

9.6. LIFE'S A JOURNEY

Life is far from straightforward, devoid of the strict logic and predictability of a computer's programs and calculations. Instead, it's a journey of ups and downs that we learn and grow from. Our society bombards us with messages about what we should eat and when we should eat it. Peer pressure, even if it's not always acknowledged, is more pervasive than we might realise. Have you met people who believe you should achieve certain milestones by specific ages, such as losing your virginity, owning a car, getting married or finding a job? Have you felt the peer pressure to fit in with the "cool kids" and be liked by everyone?

The pressure to meet expectations often causes us to forget to live life at our own pace. We are expected to rush full speed ahead, constantly striving to exceed expectations. This pressure to be what others want us to be can cause us to lose sight of who we really are. It's important to take things slowly and carefully. Rushing or taking shortcuts may cause what we desire to break along the way. It's tempting to try and please others by achieving goals, but we should never sacrifice our own satisfaction to please others who only value us for our achievements, not our true selves. Although we will encounter others on our life journey, we must establish respectable boundaries that allow us to grow and develop our own unique story. The challenges we face will help us grow stronger and inspire others to stay true to themselves. While we may face moments of solitude, these moments will test our inner strength, and with wisdom and strength we gain from this solitude, we can overcome any obstacle. Relying on others for our happiness is an unstable foundation because people will inevitably disrespect us, betray us, lie to us or abandon us during our life's journey. We often become emotionally attached to those we have spent time with and have created memories with, but when they leave or turn on us, it can feel like a deep wound. It may seem like we have given so much of ourselves to others that there is nothing left for us. However, it is possible to rebuild oneself after losing people we care about. Our identity is not dependent on others; it is within ourselves. We should take the time to remind ourselves of our inner strength to become our own person with a unique story and flavour.

To connect with your self and your inner child, reflect on experiences that made you feel strong, courageous and confident. Perhaps it was the lyrics of a song, a TV show or film, or a cherished childhood memory. Keep those thoughts and experiences close to you and draw strength from them when facing challenges. As a film enthusiast and Marvel fan, characters like Iron Man and Spider-Man have inspired me to always strive for my best, do what's right, and help those around me. Their perseverance in the face of adversity has also taught me to be strong during tough times. I believe everyone can use their passions and interests to grow and flourish as individuals. We all make mistakes, but it's our ability to persevere that makes us shine. The right balance of alone time and social interaction can help you determine what you want to achieve on your life journey and discover your life's purpose. Without a purpose, life can become dull and lack motivation, leading to a cycle of seeking short-term pleasures that can turn into addictions if not managed properly. A clear purpose, however, can provide the motivation to shine and achieve something truly remarkable, creating a sense of solid identity and belief in your abilities. Take time to explore the world around you and open your heart and mind to new experiences. Remember, life is a journey, not just a destination. The pursuit of material possessions alone will not bring true satisfaction. Instead, focus on discovering your gifts and talents and using them to build a better world and bring happiness to yourself and those around you. Everyone has something to offer, and it's up to us to choose how we use our gifts.

To share about my personal statement, I want to talk about my decision to become a Christian at the age of 17. After experiencing trauma and loneliness in my childhood, I often questioned my life direction. But when I found myself in a space where I could think clearly, I felt a strong calling that led me in a new direction. Interestingly, this new direction brought me closer to my Nana, who had recently passed away. It felt like something supernatural was reaching out to me, and when I picked the Bible out of curiosity, I felt my spirit being lifted as I looked into the subject of God. I felt like I could honour my Nana by pursuing Christianity and it was the best decision I ever made. Now, I believe that my identity is rooted in God (Father in Heaven), with Jesus as my personal guide in life to be the light and salt (The Bible - Matthew 5:14) that he calls me to be. The best thing about God is that he's eternal, as is his love (The Bible - Psalm 107:1). Through Jesus, I've found inner peace (The Bible - John 14:27), a life direction (The Bible - Psalm 32:8) and a sense of identity as a child of God (The Bible - 1 John 3:1). The song "Who You Say I Am - Hillsong Worship" reminds me of my identity every time I listen to it, and it fills me with a sense of freedom. While I understand that not everyone shares my beliefs, I hope that my story can inspire others to explore their own paths and find the purpose that gives them meaning and fulfilment.

10. Always and Forever

10.1. GET TO KNOW WHO YOU ARE

There is no one else who is exactly like you! This fact is supported both by science and by your personal interests. Let's start with the science: each person carries significant genetic prints that include fingerprints, eye biometrics, voice, lip shape, tongue bumps and ear profile. Interestingly, even your butt has a unique form. All of these unique characteristics are identifiers that distinguish you from others. Fingerprint identification is the most well-known and commonly used identification method. While it's unlikely that there are actual places that use butt scanners to identify people, there are many unique features of our bodies that we may not even know about.

However, your personality evolves and grows through all your life experiences, whether they are positive or negative. Positive experiences can turn us into a better or worse version of ourselves, and the same is true for negative experiences. For example, positive experiences can turn someone into an egotistical person when they get too much of what they want or into a compassionate soul when they receive a lot of love. On the other hand, negative experiences can turn someone into an emotionally unstable and aggressive individual who makes decisions based on emotions rather than logic or someone who becomes aware of their pain and trauma and uses it to give grace, love and compassion to others who are going through similar experiences. There is no predetermined outcome as everyone reacts differently to their experiences, but it's never too late to heal from your trauma. To do so, you must take a step back from the chaotic rush of daily life and genuinely explore your thoughts, beliefs and interests. This process requires significant effort, and it's crucial not to give up halfway through. If you can find the energy to care for others and your possessions, then you surely have the capacity to prioritise your own health and well-being.

You are a unique person! While you may share interests in certain topics and subjects with others, your perception and personal opinion about these subjects would slightly differ. It's possible for many people to have varying perspectives on the same topic. This diversity of viewpoints allows us to showcase our individual ways of thinking and our personal beliefs, revealing a unique picture of our true selves. In a world where we're often pressured to conform to certain standards and expectations, it's easy to lose touch with our true selves and the gifts that make us special. The corrupt dynamics of popularity, favouritism, dominance, materialism and hunger for power can push these unique traits under the rug. It can be tempting to fall into the trap of trying to fit in or gain others' approval, but it's essential to be honest with yourself and ask if you're truly happy with what you're doing. If not, it's okay! Take your time to explore and discover what truly makes you happy.

Always be true to yourself and do not sacrifice your happiness or compromise your beliefs just to fit in with others. I speak from experience - I once tried to be like people who were ignorant towards me, and it only led to my unhappiness. You will feel better sticking to your own truths, even if it means losing some people in your life. Dishonesty can only take you so far before the truth catches up and everything crumbles. Instead, focus on building your life around honesty and authenticity. Oscar Wilde once said, "Be yourself, everyone else is taken". Trying to be like someone else takes away your authenticity and uniqueness. You've been given your own mind and genetics, and you can make the most of them if you choose to do so. Amid the demands and stresses of life, it's essential to give yourself a break and connect with your inner self in a way that works for you. Take note of any habits or activities that may be detrimental to your physical or mental health and find ways to shift them into something that builds you up.

Discovering and working through your triggers and setbacks can help you triumph over past trauma and allow you to move forward. There is no shame in seeking guidance and support from others. Never let anyone or anything hinder you from using your gifts and talents to make a positive impact on the world. Remember that making mistakes is a natural part of life and doesn't diminish your worth or abilities. Be true to who you were created to be for you are fearfully and wonderfully made (The Bible - Psalm 139:14).

10.2. WATCH OUT FOR THE SIGNS ALWAYS

In our fast-paced and competitive world, where success often comes at the expense of others' well-being and contentment, it's crucial to stay alert. I've faced various manipulation tactics from adversaries, including guilt-tripping, where you are made to feel bad for being yourself or for having your own thoughts and beliefs. Common tactics like gaslighting, yelling and shaming are ways that people might try to coerce you into conforming to their expectations or doing something for their benefit. These tactics are designed to instil fear in you such that the next time you experience them, your body's natural response is to comply with your enemy's demands out of fear. Remember that your enemies won't reciprocate your kindness or respect. It's not worth sacrificing your dignity or individuality for someone who won't value or recognise it.

When it comes to those who try to instil fear in you to get what they want, your sense of self-worth is your strongest tool. Recognise that you are valuable, unique and deserving of love. By anchoring yourself in a strong sense of who you are and surrounding yourself with people who accept and love you for who you are, you can cultivate the confidence and inner strength to not take to heart any insults hurled your way by your enemies. These enemies can come in various forms, from blood relatives to strangers, and even friends whose perceptions of you may have changed over time causing conflicts. To guard against manipulation tactics, arm yourself with knowledge and wisdom so that you can spot the use of these tactics against you. Tactics like lying in the face of clear evidence, evading answers or projecting someone else's insecurities onto you and making you believe that your beliefs are invalid or non-existent are all designed to pull you away from your true self and your inner happiness. Your enemies may be threatened by your happiness and try to take it away from you. Don't let them! Remember that you are stronger than their attempts to bring you down. Your enemies may also criticise and shame you because they want what you have but can't have it. Their goal is either to take it from you or make you feel guilty for having it. Lying is a particularly insidious tactic that many people use today, whether to cover up a small mistake or hide a large crime. Some people even use lies to boost their own image or destroy others. I've personally experienced a lot of deceit in today's society. Many people have become so comfortable with lying that they don't want to hear the truth because it's uncomfortable. Stick to your truth and don't let others convince you that what you saw or experienced was just your imagination.

When faced with our enemies who use manipulation tactics; it's common to question not only your reality but also your very sense of self, leading to doubts about your worth and abilities. However, it's important to remind yourself of who you are and the unique abilities that give you strength to achieve your goals. I strongly recommend learning how your enemies try to control you (not for personal gain but to be aware of it) and, above all, not ignoring any red flags you may see. Even if the red flag is seen in someone you have known for years, be it a family member or someone you deeply care about and want in your life, it's sometimes healthier to let go of those who don't love you enough. It may be tempting to hold onto someone because of the history you share, but unfortunately, they can turn on you if they choose to. I have experienced sudden changes in friends' attitudes, and holding onto those friendships only prolonged my state of depression. We need to learn to let go of those who threaten us, even if it means saying goodbye to a good friend. They may have been a friend in the past, but the real question is whether they are being a friend to us now.

People may appear like they have it all, but the question remains; are they truly happy? Sadly, we often hear stories of celebrities and ordinary people unexpected dying at a very pre-mature age. It is disheartening to read headlines about people who have committed suicide, but we know that they wouldn't have taken such extreme measures if they were happy. We don't always need to put on a facade to please the world. Being our authentic selves allows the right people to come into our lives, as those who accept us for who we are will naturally gravitate towards us.

However, when we project a false image, we conceal our true feelings, and if we continue to suffer in silence for too long just to impress others, our emotions may reach a breaking point and cause us to act in extreme ways. It can be scary to expose our true selves, especially the darker parts, but not everyone will hate us for it. There are those who will appreciate us for who we are. These people are like rare gems in a mine, difficult to find, but immensely valuable. There will always be people who disagree with us, but that doesn't invalidate our beliefs or mean that we should stay silent. As long as we voice our opinions with respect, we have the right to be heard. Don't stay silent because the human mind is more fragile than we may think, and our inner selves need to be expressed. If we keep suppressing our feelings and desires, we may be pushed to deadly extremes. Examples of these extremes include falling into addiction, experiencing emotional outbursts or meltdowns, cycling through periods of depression or anxiety, and, in the worst cases, engaging in self-harm or contemplating suicide. We must keep watch over our emotions and also be mindful of the world we live in today so that we don't fall into the trap of trying to please everyone at the expense of our happiness and being our true selves.

10.3. IT'S PERFECTLY NATURAL

Society often imposes strict expectations on people and shames and despises behaviour that is actually quite natural. We're constantly bombarded with messages about what we should or shouldn't be doing. As human beings, we all experience a wide range of emotions, both positive and negative. It's perfectly normal to feel things like anger, sadness, jealousy and heartbreak. This applies to both men and women, despite the societal norms and stereotypes that exist around how each gender is supposed to express themselves. Unfortunately, there are some people who view men being emotional or crying as unattractive or weak. This is a sign that society has conditioned us to expect men to suppress their emotions. Although women are also judged for their emotional expression, the scrutiny surrounding men is particularly noticeable for me.

As a man, I have empathised with other men who have had their emotions dismissed. I've noticed that women tend to speak more openly about their emotions from the heart, while men do not do it as often. It can almost never happen. I have always been a sensitive individual, so I am acutely aware of the emotions within me. When I observed that other men didn't express their emotions as much as I did, I started to wonder if men have been quietly suffering more than we realise. It's essential for all of us to have a healthy outlet for our emotions to prevent them from becoming bottled up and leading to destructive behaviour. If we don't process our feelings in a healthy way, they can manifest in harmful ways such as physical abuse, vandalism, rebellion or even more extreme acts such as suicide or murder. So, it's essential to acknowledge that it's okay to feel sad, regardless of gender. Sadness is a natural emotion that should be accepted just as much as happiness.

Our true strength isn't demonstrated by the number of emotions we have, but by how we manage them safely to avoid causing harm to people or things. It's inevitable that we will experience pain in our lives, and it's natural to feel hurt by others. However, when we're hurt, we may be tempted to label or insult the person who caused us pain. While venting emotions can provide temporary relief, it doesn't address the root cause of our pain. Moreover, it can lead to a negative emotional spiral that's difficult to break free from. Instead, we should strive to process our pain and release it in a healthy way. When we do this, our anger will subside and we will feel more at peace. With a strong sense of inner peace and self-worth, insults from abusers will feel insignificant.

In my personal life, some people have assumed that I'm gay because I'm always very happy and enthusiastic. However, when I corrected them and said that I'm straight, they cited my perpetual happiness as the reason for their assumption. When I asked, "Are you saying that heterosexual men are incapable of being happy?" they had no response. I believe that anyone can experience deep happiness and share their emotions openly. To do so, we must resist the temptation to judge people based on superficial traits or first impressions. We should take the time to get to know people for who they truly are and show patience and understanding. This is how we can create a more loving and respectful society. After all, we wouldn't want to be judged solely based on our appearance or a brief encounter, and we should extend the same courtesy to others.

Vulnerability is a delicate subject, as it encompasses our most delicate emotions. However, vulnerability is a much more valuable asset than we give it credit for. It is only through vulnerability that we open the doors to the love we want to feel. Many of us like to put on the "tough guy" act, and sometimes we need to be strong to fight the battles that help us grow. We're not super-bots, gods or lizards who can regenerate their body parts when they lose them. We're human beings - fleshy, emotional creatures who, in all circumstances, seek to be noticed and loved. We have weaknesses, our hearts can be broken, and our emotions can tear us apart, yet we all long to feel safe in this dangerous world. Vulnerability can reveal our weaknesses and expose what causes us to break; it also enables the greatest depths of love to enter our hearts, making us feel that we are truly valuable. Vulnerability is the key to experiencing many emotions, both positive and negative, such as: empathy, trust, creativity, equity, love, joy, shame, scarcity, fear, anxiety and uncertainty. Taking a chance on love can entail the risk of feeling anxiety and grief, but does that mean that should shut down love as a result? Absolutely not! While shutting down vulnerability can be a common defence mechanism for those who have suffered severe trauma, the trauma can never be healed unless we let love in.

To do that, we have to be vulnerable. Love is the antidote of fear, so if fear is the disease, love is the cure. Pain and discomfort are an inevitable part of the human journey.

Trauma, hate, and deep pain are all a part of this journey, but there is always a place of love for us. Finding that place may require some searching and venturing, but we were made to feel love and to be loved. We should allow ourselves to feel everything we need to feel, both the positive and negative. We should not let the fear of rejection and pain be obstacles to the love we are searching for. Our weaknesses can turn into strengths, and our defeats can redirect us towards victory. It can be scary to be vulnerable in this tough world, but the right people will love our vulnerability. Deep connections, which we all need, can blossom forth when we allow ourselves to be vulnerable. Whether male or female, it is essential not to deny or reject our vulnerability, as it is a fundamental part of our humanity. If we do not allow depth into our hearts, we will never be able to experience the depth of love that we want to feel. So, let's keep our hearts open and allow love to enter.

10.4. TAKE CARE OF YOURSELF

The title above may seem like an invitation to live a selfish lifestyle, one where you indulge in luxuries and treasures without any regard for others. However, that is not what I mean at all. Taking care of ourselves is important, but so is taking care of others. It's all about finding the right balance. For instance, if a friend or family member is struggling and you know you can help them out with love and kindness, that's a selfless act that the world needs more of. We all need love and support from those around us because, as humans, we are wired to connect with others. This means that when it comes to healing from trauma, making room for comfort, replenishing your health, and rewarding yourself after a long day at work, its okay to prioritise our own needs and desires from time to time. Everyone should learn how to take care of themselves and be self-sufficient. Depending on others often can be risky, as not everyone will stick around, even if they promise to. While it's okay to accept help when needed, it's also crucial to ensure that we can take care of ourselves and sustain our own needs. It's important to recognise when we need to take a break to relieve stress and acknowledge that we are entitled to that break without feeling guilty. Prioritising self-care can help us recharge and perform at our best. When refuelling, it's crucial to engage in healthy activities that promote physical, emotional and mental wellbeing.

For some of us, when we see a family member, friend or group of people we love going through a difficult time, we can feel a deep sense of empathy and a strong desire to help them. However, it's important to remember that we can only support them and not interfere with their actions. Even when we have successfully pulled ourselves out of a tough situation, we cannot always do the same for others. It's natural to feel empathy and the urge to help, but we must recognise that we cannot help everyone and that there are limits to what we can do. When I first started my trauma healing journey with the Empath Academy, one of the most important lessons I learned was that we can support others, but we cannot fix them.

Fixing involves taking over someone else's life and actions, going too far in trying to change them for the better, to the point where we neglect our own lives. It can mean taking things away from them or enforcing things on them, which crosses a line because people need to learn how to take care of their own lives while we take care of ours. Sometimes people may not want us to interfere, and we can't fix someone who keeps falling back into their dark place or pulling us in with them. It's like trying to prop up a building or structure that doesn't have the integrity to stand on its own - we need to stand clear of the demolition zone. Supporting, on the other hand, is when someone is actively putting in the work to better their lives and progress can be seen. When we put in the hard work, we can become overwhelmed and tired, and it's okay to ask for comfort and love from our support circle. They can give us the energy and motivation to keep going, and a moment of rest with them can re-strengthen us to continue until we reach our goals.

Recognising the difference between fixing and supporting can help establish a balance between helping others and ourselves. When it comes to personal growth and development, it's important to focus your energy and efforts on your own progress rather than trying to control or change others. We all face obstacles and setbacks, but with effort, time and patience, we can overcome them and achieve our goals. It's important to be kind and patient with ourselves, even for the small steps we take towards improvement. Most importantly, while we work on ourselves, we should not compromise our personality to fit in with others. Our unique personality comes with its own set of skills, talents and abilities, which should be celebrated and not suppressed to please others. Trying to change ourselves to gain acceptance will not lead to true happiness. Instead, we should surround ourselves with the right people who appreciate us for who we are.

There will be people who always take something from you without giving back. They may seek your time, help and love, but never offer anything in return. When this happens, you may feel emotionally drained and notice an imbalance in the relationship. It's essential to establish healthy boundaries in these situations to ensure that you are taking care of yourself and not taking on any more negative energy. While we may not realise it, listening to someone vent can cause us to take on more than we are capable of handling, leaving us feeling overwhelmed. Therefore, I encourage you to pay close attention to your interactions with others, identify where to draw the line, and prioritise your own needs when necessary.

Fill your mind with wisdom to help you set boundaries and differentiate between emotionally unhealthy and healthy relationships. Additionally, don't allow others to dictate or control who you should be. You'll never fit someone else's image of you, but only your own. The following quote is from a Marvel film that I love:

Everyone fails at who they're supposed to be. The measure of a person, of a hero, is how well they succeed at being who they are.

(Avengers: Endgame, 2019)

10.5. THE ANSWER IS LOVE

Have you ever heard the phrase "Love makes the world go round"? Figuratively, this is true, but love is also the essential energy that prevents any relationship, group or community from tearing itself apart or destroying the world. Without love, it's clear that humanity would not survive. However, I'm not talking about love for material possessions, personal desires or the self. I am specifically talking about selfless, unconditional love for those around us. We are all seeking love in this world, and we all want to be loved deeply. There is nothing wrong with seeking love since we need it to survive. Deep down, when we seek love, what we truly want is to be loved not for the good things we can do, but to be loved despite our flaws and setbacks. Of course, these flaws and setbacks can be risky to reveal, especially in a judgmental world like the one we live in. It can be scary, and I've been there countless times. In our world, there is an insatiable desire for attention and followers, as evidenced by social media. While some people use social media to build up their business, there is an undeniable dynamic where people seek personal validation through accumulating followers and friends.

While it's okay to have a good number of friends, what we truly yearn for on the deepest level is love. However, this cannot be achieved by simply getting lots of people to like us. It requires a more intimate approach, where we are open and vulnerable, and share the true parts of ourselves. By doing so, we allow others to get to know us for who we truly are. Although there is a risk in exposing our weaknesses and vulnerability, it is important to spend time with the right people and observe how they treat us with respect. When we feel ready, we can begin to share the deeper parts of ourselves, one little piece at a time. This is what initiates deeper connections with our friends and helps us feel the love we need on a profound level. Revealing our true selves can be risky, but life is all about taking risks and making changes. We may win or lose, but when we do lose, something better often comes our way. So, in a sense, we never truly lose. If we are looking for intimate love, we should not mindlessly seek it through strangers. Instead, we should find love in our closest circle of friends who know everything about us accept us for who we are. We need to keep our hearts open and not be afraid to take a chance. By being our true selves and not putting on an act, we can attract people who will truly love us into our lives.

Love is not just about receiving but also about giving. Every individual possesses the ability to give love, and there are many people who are in need of it. Every day presents opportunities, both big and small, to demonstrate acts of love that can make someone's day. Whether it's a stranger, a colleague, a friend or a family member, acts of love can range from holding a door open to buying a present, from cooking a meal to spending time to help someone in need. Even the smallest acts of love can be remembered for a lifetime. For example, during my university days, when I was working at a supermarket, a random customer shouted "bless you" after I sneezed. I didn't often receive "bless you's"; hence, that small act of kindness stuck with me. Another example is when I was walking to my university's Christian Union meeting, and a group of guys greeted me and complimented me from a distance. Again, I had no idea who they were, but that random act of kindness has stayed with me for years. Unfortunately, our society is often so engrossed in electronic devices that we fail to look up and appreciate the world around us. We cannot fathom the positive impact we could have on the world if we shift our attention away from our own lives and begin to recognise and appreciate others. It is easy to become so caught up in our own affairs that we miss opportunities to both add to and benefit from the lives of others. By simply looking up and around every now and then, we may be able to answer someone's prayer or bring a ray of sunshine into their dark and depressing world. By showing someone even a small amount of love, we can lead them to a happier and livelier state of mind and heart. With enough love, they may be inspired to pass it on to others, creating a ripple effect of love that can spread throughout the world.

We all desire to be loved for who we are, and while some individuals such as film stars, artists and sports players receive an abundance of love and attention, there are others who may not have much love in their lives. This could be due to factors such as having no friends, no family or being surrounded by people who use them. Some individuals may be in prison, institutions or care homes where they receive few visitors and may be judged based on their current circumstances or past mistakes. The distribution of love in the world is definitely imbalanced, with some receiving a surplus of it, while others receive none. Showing them love is the most effective way to bring them out of a state of fear and into a more peaceful state of mind. For some, the concept of unconditional love may be foreign to them, unless it is demonstrated in their lives. The opportunities to spread love are endless and always present.

Humanity's longevity depends on our ability to support one another. Unconditional love can be challenging to practise, as we often expect love to be reciprocated. However, giving without the expectation of receiving anything in return is the most profound expression of humanity. This is the kind of love that the world needs. This kind of love is freely given, without conditions, and it is a testament to the value of the receiver. Strive for balance in giving and receiving love, while reserving enough capacity to give without expectation. Although it may be easier said than done, especially for someone like myself who still struggles with this concept, showing authentic love to those who have experienced abuse, rejection, and oppression may save them from giving up on life altogether. Different people may have various perceptions of what love looks like, but I found a great list of love traits in the Bible. 1 Corinthians 13:4-8 says, "Love is patient, love is kind. It does not envy, it does not boast, it is not proud. It does not dishonour others, it is not self-seeking, it is not easily angered, it keeps no record of wrongs. Love does not delight in evil but rejoices with the truth. It always protects, always trusts, always hopes, and always perseveres. Love never fails." We can become beacons of love in this dark world by embodying these traits. Love isn't about what we can gain for ourselves or what pleases us, but it's about giving to those around us to make others happy and considering the feelings of others. An 80's film I love shows a sentient computer summarising great love:

Love is Give and Not Take.

(Electric Dreams, 1984)

10.6. KEEP GOING, UNTIL THE END OF THE LINE

Life on this earth is a journey with its share of enjoyable moments and challenges. We are bound to experience the extremes of both. In every high and low, trial and storm, joy and accomplishment, there will be an overarching test that will determine the success of our lives. By success, I do not mean materialistic, financial or professional success (although they can be nice to have), but the greatest success in life is being the best version of oneself. It is a state where one's natural-born talents flourish, where one is not dependent on things and people for core happiness (as it is difficult to find anything or anyone that stays in one's life forever), and where one has a strong will such that the mind is not easily swayed by whatever life throws one's way. There will be people who may try to turn you into their version of you instead of accepting who you truly are. We should not conform to other people's ideas of who we are, especially when we have our own minds to decide what's best for us. In my experience, the greatest strength lies in not only staying true to ourselves but also spreading light in this dark world, more so when we don't expect anything in return. This is an element of unconditional love because it's a love that doesn't come with any debts.

Throughout life, we are guaranteed to face both triumphs and tribulations. We may win or lose, sink or swim, succeed or fail. However, as long as we keep trying, we will never fail in the true sense of the term.

As the saying goes, "Quitters never win, and winners never quit." Even in the face of losing a loved one or cherished possession, we must remember that we still possess the strength to keep moving forward. If someone tries to convince us otherwise, especially if they fail to respect our emotions, we should not let their words hold us back. Rather, the love and support of true friends and family will empower us to rise above life's challenges and succeed. I believe there are two fundamental ways to approach life: with love or with fear. If you are being mistreated by someone who is not showing any signs of love, it may seem like they are just angry. However, in reality, they are likely acting out of fear: fear of vulnerability, fear of failure, fear of embarrassment or fear of losing power. As my faith has taught me, perfect love drives out fear (The Bible - 1 John 4:18). Love is always more powerful than fear. Therefore, if you are operating from a place of love, and the person opposite you is driven by fear, you are the stronger person. Choose love over fear, and in the face of confrontation, stand firm in your worth. Remember, your value is not based on what your abusers tell you, but on how you see yourself and how your closest friends view you.

Life may not always give us what we desire, but we can be certain that we will never have absolutely nothing. We were not designed to survive in this world all by ourselves. If you can identify a few people who you know you can turn to in troubled times without any doubt or hesitation, then you will always have someone by your side. We should be grateful for the basic things we have, like a roof over our heads, a bed to sleep on, money to buy food and water, the support of people we can turn to, and even our mental, emotional, and physical health. When we don't get what we want or someone close to us betrays us, we must carefully acknowledge the emotions we are feeling and allow ourselves to process them. However, we must also focus on what we still have with us. We are only humans, and regardless of our gender, we all experience a full range of emotions. By practising an attitude of gratitude, we can stay grounded, and avoid dwelling on negative emotions for too long. This will ultimately lead to greater happiness in life.

The following are a list of the life areas addressed in this book where you will encounter difficulties in remaining true to who you are:

- With your family
- With your friends
- At your workplace or at school
- In society
- When people abuse you
- When people ignore you
- As you encounter the outside world
- As you question yourself
- When no one is around you

Some areas of life may be more challenging than others, depending on our natural talents. While we may excel in one area, we may struggle in another, and that's okay. Not everyone has to be perfect, despite what others may tell you. We didn't come into this world to be perfect, but rather to learn and develop. For those of us who are sensitive, we may tend to be overly self-critical, especially when we make mistakes or experience failure. However, it's important to remember to forgive ourselves. Everyone makes mistakes, and we are all constantly learning and growing. As long as we keep trying to do our best, we are on the right track to becoming the best version of ourselves.

So, what do you currently know about yourself? Would you say you're very comfortable with who you are? Can you say with certainty that your family and friends know who you are? How happy are you in life? Think about that for a while. How would you rate your level of happiness in life on a scale of 1-10, with 10 being the highest level of happiness? What factors are contributing to a lower number on the scale, and do you feel comfortable sharing these with someone? Who is the person you trust most to confide in? Are you willing to take the necessary steps to improve your happiness? The first step towards inner freedom is acknowledging that you need to remove toxic people from your life, make sacrifices and detach from unhealthy attachments. This involves breaking cycles that you may have been stuck in for a long time. If you have expressed annoyance or anger about a situation, then you have already voiced what you want to do. It is time for your actions to reflect your words. Your true friends, who care about your well-being, will encourage you to stay away from anything that hurts you. While it may be tempting to wait for someone to change for the better or to try to change them yourself, the results you desire will not come by staying around someone who disrespects you. It is not healthy for either of you. It is not your responsibility to alter someone's mentality; the only mind you have the power to change is your own. Although the work may be difficult, the rewards will be worth it in the end.

As we come to the end of this book, I want to express my hope that you have discovered some valuable insights that can aid you in cultivating a happier and more liberated state of mind. Breaking cycles and freeing yourself from the voices that seek to control you can be a daunting task, but it is one that is worth undertaking. We all need love, and I hope you can find the kind of love where you are not mistreated or neglected. You are a unique and wonderful person with a wealth of untapped potential. Remember that there is no one else who is exactly like you, and don't let anyone tell you otherwise. Take time to focus on the positive aspects of life and to practise self-affirmation until it becomes second nature. This positive outlook can serve as a shield to protect you when faced with challenges. While you can always support and demonstrate unconditional love to others, be cautious about how connected you become with people who aren't the best influence. Preserve the goodness within you and remain vulnerable, as it is through vulnerability that you can experience the deepest levels of love. Finally, I want to remind you that your identity is not contingent upon external factors, such as people or possessions that may leave your life at any given moment. Your identity comes from within, and the only constant in your life is yourself. Embrace your true self and live your life to the fullest.

I encourage you to keep exploring, growing and loving. You are not here by accident, and your life is not a coincidence. Every moment is a chance to become a better version of yourself and find the love you seek. As the Bible states in Philippians 4:8, "Whatever is true, whatever is noble, whatever is right, whatever is pure, whatever is lovely, whatever is admirable, if anything is excellent or praiseworthy, think about such things." By focusing on the good, you can live a life of pure joy. Your life is precious, and you should take care of yourself. Discover your skills and talents, and use them to make a positive impact on the world. Don't be consumed by the digital world; take your eyes off the phone screen and observe the world around you. Above all, in every trial, storm, heartbreak and tough situation, I encourage you to do one thing... stay true to you!

References and Sources

- *The Bible - New International Version*
- The Empath Academy (2020) https://www.facebook.com/groups/myempathacademy
- Lindsay C. Gibson (2015) *Adult Children of Emotionally Immature Parents: How to Heal from Distant, Rejecting, or Self-Involved Parents.* Oakland, California: New Harbinger Publications, Inc.
- John Gray (2005) *Men are from Mars, Women are from Venus.* London: Collins Educational.
- Anodea Judith (2016) *Wheels of Life: A User's Guide to the Chakra System.* Woodbury, Minnesota: Llewellyn Publications.
- Gary Chapman (2017) *The 5 Love Languages Singles Edition.* Moody Publishers.
- Rachel Jones (2019) *Is This It?* The Good Book Company.
- Marianne Williamson (2015) *A Return to Love: Reflections on the Principles of a Course in Miracles.* London: Thorsons Classics.
- Vaughan Roberts (2007) *Battles Christians Face.* Milton Keynes, England: Authentic Media Inc.
- Richard J. Foster (1985) *Money, Sex & Power: The challenge of the disciplined life.* London: Hodder & Stoughton.

- Steve Peters (2013) *The Chimp Paradox: The Mind Management Programme for Confidence, Success, and Happiness*. London: Vermilion.
- Brene Brown: *The Call to Courage*. Netflix.com (2019)
- *Teal Swan* YouTube Channel (2022).
- *Lilo and Stitch* Dir. by Chris Sanders & Dean DeBlois (Walt Disney Pictures, 2002)
- *The Lion King* Dir. by Roger Allers & Rob Minkoff (Walt Disney Pictures, 1994)
- *WandaVision* Dir. by Matt Shakman (Marvel Studios, 2021)[Disney+]
- *Avengers Endgame* Dir. by Anthony and Joe Russo (Marvel Studios, 2019)
- *Lilo and Stitch: The Series* Created by Walt Disney Television Animation, Disney Channel (2003-2006)
- *Brooklyn Nine-Nine* Created by Dan Goor & Michael Schur, Fremulon, Dr Good Productions, 3 Arts Entertainment Universal Television (2013-2021)
- *Mean Girls* Dir. by Mark Waters (Paramount Pictures, 2004)
- *The Incredibles* Dir. by Brad Bird (Walt Disney Pictures, Pixar Animation Studios, 2004)
- *Back to the Future* Dir. by Robert Zemeckis (Universal Pictures, 1985)

- *Back to the Future Part III* Dir. by Robert Zemeckis (Universal Pictures, 1990)
- *High School Musical* Dir. by Kenny Ortega (Disney Channel, 2006)[Disney Channel]
- *Spider-Man 3* Dir. by Sam Raimi (Columbia Pictures, Marvel Entertainment, Laura Ziskin Prod. 2007)
- *Titanic* Dir. by James Cameron (Paramount Pictures, 20th Century Fox, Lightstorm Ent. 1997)
- *Electric Dreams* Dir. by Steve Barron (Virgin Pictures Ltd, 1984)
- The Rembrandts (1995) "I'll Be There For You". Gavin MacKillop
- Taylor Swift (2014) "Shake it Off". Max Martin and Shellback
- Sara Bareilles (2013) "Brave". Mark Endert
- Kelly Clarkson (2012) "Stronger (What Doesn't Kill You)". Greg Kurstin
- Rachel Patten (2014) "Fight Song". Jon Levine
- Ava Max (2019) "So Am I". Cirkut

Printed in Great Britain
by Amazon